Corrie ten Boom

Sam Wellman

© MCMXCVII by Sam Wellman

ISBN 1-55748-956-4

Published by Barbour & Company, Inc.
          P.O. Box 719
          Uhrichsville, Ohio 44683
          http://www.barbourbooks.com

ᴇᴄᴘᴀ Member of the
Evangelical Christian
Publishers Association

Printed in the United States of America.

CHAPTER 1

The vaporizer on the small alcohol stove spewed a fog of camphor and water into the air of the dark bedroom. The vapor clouded over Corrie ten Boom, who clutched a blanket over herself on a bed. Aches shadowed every movement of her body.

"Dear Jesus," she prayed, "let this pass."

Corrie ten Boom felt her years. It seemed as if until today she had never stopped long enough in all her fifty-one years to let age catch up with her. But more than age caught up with her today. Her prayer was a plea for many things to pass. Jesus had been in her heart for a very long time and she hoped her fear was just momentary, just another unpleasant symptom of the flu.

"But everything has gone wrong lately," she muttered.

It seemed everyone in Holland must know the ten Booms were hiding fugitives in their house. After all, it was 1944. Holland had been infested by German soldiers four years. Worst of all the Germans were the slithery Gestapo, the secret police of the Nazis. The ten Booms had been hiding Jews and Dutch boys in their house for two years. They never had less than seven fugitives living with them these desperate days. How much longer could their secret last before the dreaded Gestapo bashed on their door? The Gestapo struck at night like vipers. Their victims were groggy, unprepared—like Corrie felt now.

"Is it night or day?" She tried to focus her eyes.

She had slept in this very same bedroom in this very same house as long as she could remember. Her home was so precious to her. The past was so wonderful that thinking about it softened her pain. Her thoughts drifted back. . . .

Yes. As far back as she could remember her home was *gezellig:* "close and warm and cozy"—smelling of soup and fresh bread, and sounding of soft laughter and the rustles of Mama and three Aunts in long dresses. A five-year-old like Corrie could have a wonderful party with her doll Casperina under the dining room table. She could even creep down the steps into Papa's work room behind his shop that faced Barteljorisstraat. Silently she sat and smelled his cigar and listened to clocks ticking and tocking like hundreds of heartbeats. She watched bearded Papa bent over his bench. God must have been right there with him.

Each time Papa placed some tiny thing in a watch he would pause to say, "Thank You, Lord," as gently as if he were talking to Corrie or Mama.

Corrie, her two sisters and brother were the best of friends. Betsie was seven years older than Corrie, Willem five and Nollie two. Betsie was a sleepy-eyed beauty, but was convinced she could never marry. She had anemia. Marriage would destroy her. She resolved to stay at home and help Papa in the shop. Willem was witty, but often lapsed serious, even gloomy. Of all the children Nollie was the most "normal," rarely ill or in trouble. For years it was Nollie—the *moedertje*, the "little mother"—who played with Corrie.

Nollie was entrusted to take Corrie down the narrow sidewalk on Barteljorisstraat. Within minutes they saw the

Gothic spire of Saint Bavo's Cathedral towering over the town square. The girls would find a bench and watch grownups strolling through the square or hurrying to a horse-drawn trolley. Many people bustled in and out of shops of all kinds. Nestled against Saint Bavo's was the fish market. Across a tiny street was the butcher's hall. On one side of the square was the Town Hall. Three times a week the area was choked with farmers clopping around in wooden *klompen,* selling fruit and vegetables to the women of Haarlem in long black dresses and black bonnets.

Nollie would say, "Papa said our Dutch farmers are like no other farmers in the world. They took their land from the very sea."

Sometimes the sisters would find cousin Dot who lived next to Saint Bavo's and sneak inside the great cathedral. Uncle Arnold was an usher there. Below a colossal golden organ they played hide and seek in the pews. Sometimes they left the square to venture a short way down Damstraat to the Spaarne River. It was a bouquet of colorful boats. Their pilots bragged they could take Corrie anyplace in Holland on a boat. She believed them. She couldn't go more than a few blocks from home in any direction without coming to a canal or the river. And of course if Papa walked her west of Haarlem, in not much more than an hour's time she faced the mighty North Sea.

But it was in the home Corrie found peace. Mama, in spite of living in white-knuckled pain from gallstones, was the peacemaker. It was Mama who understood in a flash what was in someone's mind and was smoothing things over before anyone else even realized what was happening. It was Mama who knitted baby clothes or wrote cheery messages for shut-ins—often from her invalid's bed!

And then there was Papa, called by many the best

watchmaker in Holland, so skilled that young men came from all over Europe to ask to apprentice with him. Papa would always try to accommodate them. But he was so much more than a superb watchmaker. How he loved the Jews, God's chosen people. He came from a long line of ten Booms who were never afraid to take God's side as revealed in the Bible. Papa's grandfather Gerrit lost his job as a gardener because he spoke up against the dictator Napoleon. Papa's father, Willem, the original watchmaker at Barteljorisstraat, started a Society for Israel, a fellowship to pray for the Jews.

"Jews are the apple of God's eye," was heard often among the ten Booms.

Papa's love of the Jews matured in his first years as a watchmaker in the poor Jewish section of Amsterdam. He read the Old Testament—their Talmud—with them and even celebrated their Sabbath and holy days. His fifteen years in Amsterdam bore much fruit. He met Mama there. All the ten Boom children were born there. Aunt Anna and Aunt Bep were already living with him in Amsterdam. Then Papa had to return to Haarlem. His father Willem had died and his mother needed help with the shop. His mother died. Then a third aunt, Aunt Jans, came to live with them.

Papa took God's love and loved everyone in return. Like Jesus he told parables for many occasions. Often, Corrie went with Papa on the train to Amsterdam where he bought watch parts and also carried back the official time from the Naval Observatory. One day she told Papa she was afraid someone in the family would die. After all, Mama and Aunt Jans and Aunt Bep were all sick a lot.

"How could I ever bear such pain?" she asked Papa.

CHAPTER 2

Papa asked her, "When we take the train to Amsterdam, when do I give you the ticket?"

"Just before we get on the train."

"And so God will give you the courage to carry the pain when the time comes for someone to die. Until then you should not carry the pain. God does not want you to."

Before and *after* every meal Papa would ask God to bless the Queen of Holland and end grace with "let soon come the day that Jesus, your beloved Son, comes on the clouds of heaven. Amen." He never stopped reminding everyone that Christ was going to return.

"A penny in the blessing box for your coming," gushed Mama when guests arrived, and she would put a penny for the missionaries in a small metal box in the dining room. Every time the family was blessed in some way this was her way of showing thanks to God. The guests were very flattered too, because the ten Booms did not have an abundance of pennies. Guests would bring flutes and violins and other instruments to play in Aunt Jans's front room where she had an upright piano. Aunt Jans even began inviting soldiers she saw loitering in the streets.

"They look so lonely," she said.

Soon Aunt Jans organized a soldier's center and raised funds for a building of their own. She went there herself to give Bible lessons and sing hymns. Corrie sang there too—even solos.

It seemed every member of the family was a natural organizer. Aunt Anna organized a club for servant girls. The poor innocents needed encouragement. They were often alone and preyed upon. Every Wednesday she would meet with her girls for Bible study and hymns. And if one of her girls got in "trouble" Aunt Anna couldn't have been more heartbroken if the girl were her own daughter.

Papa organized too. He published a little magazine for watchmakers. He was always involved in civic events like the annual parade for the Queen's birthday. And every week when he visited the houses of rich Haarlemites to wind their clocks he would adjourn afterwards with the servants for Bible lessons. One just couldn't live in Christ without wanting to help one and all. To love was to serve.

"And sometimes it is necessary to organize to get started," Papa told Corrie.

As Corrie became older she realized only too well how Betsie and Nollie turned the heads of boys. But not Corrie—the pretty little girl lengthened and strengthened in all the wrong places. She became pigeon-toed and high-hipped. Her lips were so wide and so thin they were a cartoon. Her jaw got stubborn and never softened. Her eyes, turned down on the corners, would have seemed perpetually sorrowful if she hadn't smiled so much. Such slight differences between beautiful and homely!

But as her physical appearance evolved, so had her heart. By the time Corrie was fourteen she had Jesus in her heart. She loved Holland and the Queen. She knew how to act like a lady. She had a loving family. At sixteen Corrie finished secondary school, pondering her next step. Should she go on to become a teacher like Nollie? She wasn't sure. But she plowed ahead. She began Normal

School and eagerly sought things to do outside the home. Betsie urged her to tell Bible stories to children. Her first time in front of children Corrie exhausted the story of Jesus feeding the five thousand in five minutes! Without a moment's hesitation, Betsie took up the story. She made the story come alive. Where were people sitting? Where had they come from? Did Jesus speak to them from the bottom of the hill or the top? What did the Sea of Galilee look like? What were the people thinking before the miracle? What did they think after the miracle?

After that Corrie knew how to tell a story. She gushed at Betsie, "It was as if you painted a wonderful detailed picture like one of the old masters!"

Corrie became more and more confident outside the home. Finally she left home to work as a governess for a rich family in a seashore town. Her charge, a little girl, was spoiled. But Corrie knew now how to enthrall a child with a good story. She soon won the little girl's respect and trust. But the rest of the family seemed hopeless. They were selfish and cynical. They gloated over their social superiority. They talked of nothing but money and possessions. Corrie had not visited wealthy homes before like Papa had. She didn't know if wealth caused people to behave this way or if it was just this family, fallen far away from God and the Bible. Just how far they had fallen was proved when the master of the house tried to force himself on Corrie. She escaped from him but she was miserable. She didn't want to stay. How could she remain in such sin? But she didn't want to quit either. Mustn't she sow the seed of the Gospel in the little girl? Who would save this little girl if she left?

"Please Lord, let me know what to do," she prayed.

Soon Willem appeared at the mansion. "Aunt Bep is

dead. At last her suffering is over. You must come home, Corrie. Aunt Anna is exhausted from caring for her and Mama and Aunt Jans. Betsie must help Papa in the shop. Nollie has a permanent job as a school teacher."

"I must go home then."

So the decision to leave was made for her. Or was it God's hand? But why would God let her abandon the child if hope remained? She had to trust God always. But it was painful to think of leaving the child. On the way back to Haarlem Willem began singing Bach at the top of his lungs.

"How can you sing when Aunt Bep just died?" she asked.

"A true Christian rejoices when a loved one goes to heaven to be with the Lord. Grief is an indulgence for ourselves."

Was Willem right? Corrie would have to think about it a lot more before she could bring herself to sing. Once again Corrie, at eighteen, was home. Willem had been right. Aunt Anna was worn out. Now Corrie was *the* housekeeper of the home. She didn't get comfort from the acts of cleaning house and cooking like Aunt Anna did. Her goal every day was simply to finish the work faster than she did the day before.

Mama bluntly told her, "Housework is not fulfilling for you, Corrie."

Papa said, "Yes, Corrie. You need more. What about the new Bible School that just opened in Haarlem?"

So, urged by her parents, Corrie once again attended school, attacking what seemed to be their entire curriculum at once: ethics, dogmatics, church history, Old Testament, New Testament, Old Testament history and New Testament history. For two years she studied very hard in her moments outside of housework. Then she failed her examinations. The defeat was stinging. Maybe she had attempted too much. However, she could still serve the church by teaching catechism to children. She could still prepare people for confirmation. And she could teach Bible lessons in the public schools.

"You are a good teacher, a gifted teacher," insisted Betsie.

Her setback seemed trivial compared to what was happening in Europe. Holland managed to stay neutral in the "Great War" that exploded across Europe in 1914. The awful trenches of the war threatened to grind up all the young men in France, Germany and England. Bad news flooded their home too. Mama was sicker than ever. Aunt Anna fought tuberculosis. And Aunt Jans succumbed to diabetes. When the end was near she said, "Dear Jesus, I thank You that You have done everything for us on the cross, and that all we need in life or death is to be sure of this." After years of worrying about death Aunt Jans had triumphed in a twinkling. It was just as Papa had told Corrie all her life. When the time comes, God provides for the faithful.

CHAPTER 3

Good news or bad, nothing remained the same very long with the ten Booms. Willem became a pastor. He was even married now. Mama had a stroke so severe she went into a coma. For two months around the clock they watched her in shifts: Corrie, Betsie, Anna, Papa and Nollie. And one morning Mama woke up!

"Corrie," she said.

She spoke only two other words: "yes" and "no." Corrie believed her name was one of the three words only because she was with Mama in the kitchen when she had her stroke. She recovered enough to walk again, but only with help. She could not use her hands to write or knit.

The Great War ended. Much of Europe was devastated. Papa was not interested in assigning guilt. He knew many children were destitute. As chairman of the International Watchmakers, he urged his membership to take children who had been victims of the war into their homes. The ten Boom house itself had very little money but much love. It wasn't long before the ten Booms welcomed urchins from the streets of Germany. Even Mama was up and about, fussing over the newcomers.

The next months had mixed blessings for the ten Booms. Corrie took the exam at the Bible School and passed. Nollie married Flip van Woerden, a teacher also. Then Mama died. Corrie wrestled with the injustice of Mama's suffering. Why did such a warm loving woman have to suffer like she had? Finally she decided that she had learned from Mama that love could transcend all human affliction. Her whole life Mama had shown her love by doing things for people, but in the end, with her normal expressions of love paralyzed, Mama's love still radiated, whole and complete.

"Nothing can defeat love," concluded Corrie.

Christmas time of 1920 was a great turning point for Corrie. She was twenty-eight years old. It started innocently: Betsie got the flu. So Corrie helped Papa in the shop. She greeted customers and worked with the bills and correspondence. As Betsie got better she began picking up Corrie's duties in the house. Sensitive, artistic Betsie was much better at housework than Corrie. She had a special touch, like Aunt Anna. But the reverse was true too! Corrie was much better at working in the shop than Betsie had been. God surely arranged this insight. And they each loved their new role. Without a moment's hesitation they exchanged duties.

Keeping the books and welcoming customers was not enough for Corrie. She asked Papa, "May I learn to work on watches?"

"You're the only one of the children who ever asked me that," he answered in surprise. "But if you had been the fourth I would still say 'Yes, of course you may.' I will teach you."

So Corrie, trained by the best watchmaker in Holland, became the first woman watchmaker licensed in Holland. Her specialty was the new rage: wristwatches. But even that was not enough for Corrie. She gave Bible lessons to children as always, but now had a special class for the retarded. In addition to that, a wealthy ladies' club concerned about lack of activities for teenaged girls in Haarlem enlisted Corrie and Betsie to take girls on outings.

Corrie and Betsie knew exactly how to entertain girls and still give them the real meat of such endeavors—the Gospel. It was sandwiched in the middle of fun things to do. Soon the two sisters organized an official girls' club, then branched out. It was not long before Corrie coordinated forty ladies, each with a troop of eight girls. Their 300 girls became quite a presence in Haarlem. Once a year they rented the concert hall to show a thousand friends and relatives the skills they were learning in the clubs.

"Who could have imagined in the beginning that we would do this?" Corrie asked Betsie.

Within a few years Corrie became a fearless public speaker. Always, right in the middle of the show, she offered the Gospel in talks with catchy titles like "God's telephone is never busy" or "Do You Have Your Radio Tuned to the Right Station?" Her organization, known as the Haarlem Girls' Clubs, was welcomed into the Christian Union of the Lady Friends of the Young Girl, with headquarters in Switzerland. The girls and their leaders now wore uniforms!

Another death struck the family. Aunt Anna died. Papa's house had once resounded with nine people living in seven bedrooms. Now only Papa, Betsie and Corrie remained. The war urchins had been placed with families in their homeland. Papa was not one to waste empty bedrooms. The ten Booms had bedrooms to share. And plenty of love.

Betsie said, "I remember Mama saying if we did anything to help the missionary effort besides donate a few pennies we should help the children of missionaries."

So they began to take in children left in Holland by missionaries. This was a major undertaking. These children were to be raised to adulthood. And even though they were the offspring of missionaries and usually eager to please, many were at a difficult age. The new children named the house "Beje," pronounced "bay-yay," for the initials of Bartel Joris, for whom Barteljorisstraat was named. Betsie and Corrie became their "Aunts." Papa became "Opa," Dutch for "Grandpa."

Once, before the Bible reading at supper, a child said, "Opa, let's read Psalm 117 tonight. I really like that one," trying not to smile. Psalm 117 had only twenty-nine words.

"Psalm 117?" answered Opa agreeably as he turned the pages. "Oh," he said innocently, "Let's read 119 instead." Psalm 119 had 176 verses and 2337 words! And so the children learned saintly Opa was no fool. And the Bible was to be taken very seriously.

In 1930 Papa became gravely ill, but recovered. His illness was a wake up call for the ten Booms. He was seventy years old. They had already hired a bookkeeper for the shop, a woman named Toos. Now they hired an itinerant watchmaker named Christoffels.

Papa was excited. "Don't judge him by his ragged clothing. He's the old style clock man, the kind who roams the country fixing any kind of watch or clock ever made. He will be invaluable to us."

Over the years Corrie's large organization for girls became independent again. Now it was the Triangle Club. The triangle represented social, intellectual and physical skills. But the triangle was inside a circle. This meant being in the right relationship with God. Their four club rules were:

Seek your strength through prayer.
Be open and trustworthy.

Bear your difficulties cheerfully.
Develop the gifts that God gave you.

Corrie openly embraced Christianity—but as always wisely gave girls the Gospel in small potent doses.

The 1930s seemed golden for the three ten Booms at the Beje. They successfully fostered missionary children and sent the last of them into the world. Yet, evil loomed on the eastern horizon. Since 1927 when Willem studied in Germany for his doctorate he had railed about the evil growing in Germany. It was a socialism of the most heartless kind. It called itself the National Socialist German Workers. It became known as the "Nazi" party. The poor, the old, the feebleminded, the handicapped were enemies of progress, declared the Nazis. Soon Jews were included as enemies too, then Communists.

"Surely no one believes such nonsense," said Papa.

Radios had been invented only years before. Now in the Beje family enjoyed the blissful concerts Betsie found by carefully studying the radio schedules. But once in a while as she turned the dial to search for a station the radio erupted with fiery screams from Germany that seemed straight from hell. The ranting was that of the demented mastermind behind the Nazis: Adolph Hitler.

"Surely no one believes such a devil," said Papa.

The Nazi message intruded into the Beje another way. Papa had a young German apprentice named Otto. One day he attacked Christoffels. His reason was that Christoffels was old, decrepit and worthless. Papa fired Otto immediately. Later Papa made excuses for Otto: he was young and confused. Gloomy Willem, a frequent visitor, said no—Otto was a typical German these days.

In 1939 Germany signed a peace pact with Russia.

"That is very bad," said Willem. "Hitler just made sure the Russians will stay on the sidelines. He will conquer Poland now."

One week later Germany invaded Poland. The news on the radio was heartbreaking. Hitler's tanks crushed horses of the Polish cavalry. The Germans divided Poland with Russia. The Americans declared their neutrality. Were Americans afraid to fight, like Hitler said? The French and British declared war on Germany. Which was worse? To fight or to be neutral?

"Surely we Dutch will be neutral as we were in the Great War," prayed Corrie.

"This maniac Hitler may not permit any country to stay neutral," countered Willem.

Only the French and British opposed Hitler. Fighting took place on the open seas in great naval battles. Suddenly in April of 1940 Germany invaded Norway and Denmark. Hitler explained he was protecting them from the French and British who had designs on them. Corrie remembered the summer she and her girls had hiked into Germany to tour the Rhine. It was so easy. Germany was less than 100 miles away from Haarlem. But in early May the Prime Minister of Holland came on the radio to reassure the Dutch that Holland was neutral.

Papa snapped off the volume. "I'm sorry for all the Dutch who don't know God. Because we will be attacked by the Germans and we will be defeated."

It seemed Papa, who tried to see the good in everyone and everything, had sealed their grim fate. Corrie went to bed and for the first time in her life she prayed Papa was wrong. Surely this nightmare couldn't be happening.

She awoke hours later to lightning and thunder. Noises popped and boomed and crackled. Then the whine of machines. Machines and men.

"No! That is not a thunderstorm!" cried Corrie.

She raced down the stairs and checked on Papa. He was asleep. She dashed into Betsie's bedroom. Betsie was sitting up, terrified. They hugged each other.

"Most of the big explosions seem far to the east," said Betsie. "I'll bet the Germans are bombing Amsterdam."

War!

CHAPTER 4

Corrie's world seemed plunged into hell. In the hours that followed she and Betsie prayed for Holland. Betsie even prayed for the Germans. What sisters Corrie had! Nollie could not tell a lie. And Betsie prayed for everyone, including their enemies.

"Lord, answer our prayers. . . ."

While praying, Corrie swooned. She had a vision. She couldn't have dreamed it. Who could have slept at such a time? In the town square she saw four enormous black horses pulling a farm wagon. In the wagon was Corrie herself! And Papa. And Betsie. She realized now the wagon was crowded. There were Willem and Nollie! Toos and young nephew Peter. None of them could get off the wagon. They were being taken somewhere. What could the vision mean?

The bombing stopped.

Joined by Papa, looking all of his eighty years, they listened to the radio. The radio said Germans were bombing airports all over Holland. Germans had parachuted into Rotterdam, Dordrecht and Moerdijk. . . .

"How odd," said Betsie. "Moerdijk is a tiny village."

Papa said, "No. The Germans want to capture the bridges in those three places, so their tanks can move quickly all over Holland." Dear Papa, seemingly so naive, was so wise in the affairs of men. But how could one read the Bible like he did and not know every nuance of men and their flawed ambitions?

After the dawn the Haarlemites walked the streets in a daze. They taped their windows as the radio had urged them to do, but there was little else to do. Even Papa strolled the streets. They walked through the town square. They crossed the bridge over the Spaarne. They walked to the ancient Amsterdam Gate which once sealed the city walls. They visited the great cherry tree called the Bride of Haarlem. There were no craters, no shattered windows, no crumpled bricks.

"All the bombs must have fallen on Schiphol airport at Amsterdam," observed Corrie, remembering what the radio said.

The Queen of Holland fled to England on May 13. The Dutch army collapsed into a small area from Amsterdam to Rotterdam they called "Fortress Holland," as if it were impregnable against the Nazis. Within two days "Fortress Holland" crumpled. The Dutch army surrendered. Days later German soldiers paraded into Haarlem, goose-stepping in crisp gray and black uniforms. They had tanks and cannons and trucks and half-tracks and hundreds of huge red flags, each with a black swastika inside a white circle. It was ironic that the flags reminded Corrie of her Triangle Club, except the swastika was completely at odds with God, swirling and ripping and tearing like blades of the devil.

The Dutch were assured the Germans were there to defend them against the French and British. In fact, declared the Germans, Holland was now part of the glorious German empire or "Reich."

"The Germans say their Reich will last a thousand years!" moaned Betsie.

"No. Such transparent evil can not endure," objected

Papa. "But I fear it will last a long time. . . ."

At first the occupation did not seem so evil to Corrie. German soldiers had money. They bought things at the shop. They even bought all of Papa's *winkeldochters*,—"shop daughters"—his clocks and watches that had been in the shop for years without being sold. There were a few inconveniences, such as the Dutch could not be in the street after ten o'clock at night. But what respectable citizen would be out then anyway? And each Dutch citizen had to carry an identity card in a pouch hanging from a "necklace." And food and merchandise had to be purchased with coupons from ration books. Was that so bad? The Germans were very well organized. And the Dutch could have no telephones, but heaven knows people listened to too much gossip on phones anyway. And the newspapers no longer carried any real news. Any fool realized that. But the news was depressing anyway. All of Europe was falling into the German Reich.

"This occupation is seductive," said Papa after a few weeks. "The Nazis are more patient than I thought."

When the Dutch were ordered to turn in their radios they began to be upset. They loved to listen to their concerts. But Willem insisted the Dutch must keep their radios or they would be hopelessly trapped in a world of never-ending lies and deceit. With radios they could hear the truth broadcast from England. So he convinced Corrie to turn in one radio to the Germans and lie about owning another one. She felt very bad lying. She told herself she was only being as wise and shrewd as a snake but innocent as a dove as Jesus advised one to be against a world of evil. But she didn't seek the opinion of Betsie or Papa.

Betsie chirped, "Oh, did the Nazis let us keep our other radio?" But her face fell when she realized their other radio was being hidden under the staircase.

The Dutch were not pleased about losing their bicycles either. Everyone rode bicycles. Even Corrie. It had started with German soldiers stopping riders and confiscating the tires. The tires were shipped back to Germany. Rubber was precious. The practical Dutch could understand that, even if they didn't like it. They quickly learned to wrap the rims with cloth and ride the bicycles anyway. But soon the soldiers were confiscating the bicycles. So the Nazis had more in mind. They didn't want the Dutch moving around. Soon thousands of the Dutch hid bicycles inside their homes.

Corrie's girls' clubs were banned. The Nazis were not about to allow any well organized network of 300 Dutch to exist in one town—even teenaged girls and their leaders. Who knew how such innocents might be used by an underground of traitors to the German Reich? And gradually the ten o'clock curfew was moved earlier and earlier. It wasn't long into the Nazi occupation until just being out after dark was forbidden. Night time was just too convenient for traitors to the German Reich.

The Nazis double-crossed the Russians in June of 1941 and were mangling Russian troops on a battle front east of Germany. The Nazis seemed invincible. Their occupation of western Europe displayed more evil every day. Signs appeared in Dutch shops: NO JEWS SERVED HERE. Surely those were just a few misguided anti-Semites, said Papa hopefully. But then an official sign appeared in a public park: NO JEWS ALLOWED. Soon Jews were made to wear a large yellow star of David with *Jood*, the Dutch word for "Jew," sewed inside.

Papa was dismayed. "The Jews are the apples of God's eye. I pity the Germans."

Watches left by Jews for repair in the shop began to accumulate. Were their owners afraid to come to get them? Then the watch shop of a Jewish watchmaker closed. He and his wife had vanished. Papa was stunned. The Jewish watchmaker had been there in downtown Haarlem for thirty-one years. He wouldn't just leave suddenly. The Dutch heard more and more rumors about the Gestapo. They were the secret police, supposedly the very worst of the Nazis.

More and more often they heard the roar of engines overhead at night. Was it because Haarlem was below the path of German planes flying to bomb England? One night in the summer the sky over Haarlem not only roared and whined with the noise of engines but the sky flickered with light. The fiery traces were not the paths of shooting stars but bullets! There was a battle above Haarlem. The ten Booms huddled in the dining room until the night sky was silent.

Later Corrie found a hunk of metal on her bed. "Betsie! If I had been in bed it would have struck me right in the head. . . ."

Betsie smiled patiently. "In God's world there are no "ifs." And no place is any safer than any other place. Our only safety is in the center of God's will. Let us pray that we know His will."

For a year and a half the ten Booms in the Beje tried to live their normal lives. One November morning in 1941 changed that. Corrie and Betsie watched through their shop window in horror as German soldiers smashed up Mr. Weil's shop across the street and hauled off his furs. Mr. Weil stood on the sidewalk in a daze.

"We must help him," cried Corrie.

She and Betsie ran out to quickly usher him down the

alley and up into their dining room.

"Mr. Weil!" exclaimed Papa happily, not realizing what happened. He cherished visitors.

"I must warn my wife," worried Mr. Weil. "She's visiting relatives in Amsterdam. She must not come home."

Corrie was a forty-nine-year-old watchmaker. What could she do? She mumbled, "Willem will know what to do."

As if in a dream she found herself walking north on Kruisstraat to the railway station, then riding the train through Amsterdam all the way to Hilversum. She got off the train at mid-day. A few hours later Corrie rode the train back to Haarlem. That night Willem's son Kik came for Mr. Weil and they disappeared into the dark alley.

When Corrie saw Kik two weeks later she whispered, "How are the Weils?"

"If you are going to work in the underground you must not ask questions. The less you know the less the Gestapo can torture out of you." Kik was smiling apologetically, but Corrie shivered.

So brother Willem and his son Kik were involved with the underground! And many Dutch people were now hiding Jews. Even Nollie, who now had six children of her own. She and husband Flip sheltered two Jews: a young blond woman named Annaliese, who looked very Dutch and went about freely, and Katrien, an older woman who posed as their maid. Would Jews seek refuge in the Beje? Just a few weeks later Corrie heard a desperate knock on the alley door of the Beje. She didn't hesitate a moment when she saw the fear in the visitor's eyes.

"Come inside!" She rushed a woman up to the dining room.

"I'm Mrs. Kleermacher. I'm a Jew," said the woman.

"God's people are always welcome in this house," said Papa.

"Thank God," she said. "I heard you ten Booms helped Mr. Weil." She sobbed. "My husband has already been arrested."

Two nights later an elderly Jewish couple joined Mrs. Kleermacher in hiding. The Beje could be nothing more than a rest stop. The Jews had to move on to safer places. But where? Once again she traveled to Hilversum on the train.

This time Willem said, "Most Jews work on farms. But that's getting more and more difficult. Even the farms must account for their food now. We can find places on farms if they bring food ration books with them. Otherwise. . ."

"But Jews aren't issued ration books!" cried Corrie.

"They can't be counterfeited either. The Nazis change the design too often."

"But what can we do, Willem?"

"We must steal the ration books." And he sighed as he noticed Corrie waiting expectantly. "I can't do it, Corrie. They watch me now every moment."

Corrie remembered someone. "I know a man named—"

Willem gently put a finger on her lips. "Don't tell me his name, dear Sister."

She worried all the way home on the train. There was a girl who had come to her Sunday school class for the retarded for twenty years. Her father worked at the Food Office. Could Corrie appeal to this man for help? She had sought help from people for years and years for her many projects. But never was so much at stake as now. What would the Gestapo do to this man if he were caught? And what if he were a Nazi sympathizer? What would happen to her and Betsie and Papa? Papa was so old. Never had the world seemed so evil.

"Oh please God, help me," she prayed.

She rode her bicycle to the man's house that very night. He listened to her impassively. There was no sign of sympathy. Perhaps she saw some fear. Or was it anger?

CHAPTER 5

The man who worked at the Food Office sighed. "The ration books must be accounted for a dozen ways. There is only one way to get any books for your purposes. . . ."

"Yes?" she asked hopefully.

"We must be robbed. It happens often these days with Dutch people so desperate for food. They wouldn't necessarily suspect me. How many books do you want?"

Three? No, she argued with herself, there would be other Jews fleeing. Five? How many should she ask for? He was going to be robbed. He would be grilled by the Gestapo. That sacrifice should not come cheap. "I need one hundred ration books," she said stoutly, hardly believing her own words.

A week later she visited the man again. He handed her the food ration books in an envelope. His face was raw with bruises. His friends had done it to him. He paid a heavy price for the books. Yet the Gestapo would not have believed anything less than a bloody thrashing.

"God will bless you for this," she said.

The glory of it was that the staged robbery did not have to be repeated. The last coupon in the book was presented to the Food Office for the next month's ration book. So Corrie had one hundred permanent food rations to dispense. One hundred lives saved!

One day a frail man with a goatee came to explore

the Beje. Corrie was expecting him. Like everyone in the underground he was named Smit. "This structure is a dream come true," he said. "Never have I seen such a hodgepodge of rooms."

"We prefer to think of it as unique," quipped Corrie, not bothered by his remark. She could always take criticism, even if it stung.

The structure of the home was peculiar. The front part was an old house three stories high, yet was only one room wide, that ran deep off Barteljorisstraat. It was joined behind to another old house three stories high and one room wide but just one room deep. The floors of the two houses missed each other by several feet but the mismatch was obscured by stairs in the seam between the two houses.

Corrie wasn't happy though when Mr. Smit seemed to focus on her small bedroom on the third floor. He said, "This room is perfect. It's high. It gives people time to get up here and hide as the Gestapo sweep through the lower part of the house."

"But this is my bedroom. And it's so small."

One week later Corrie's bedroom was even smaller. The man and his helpers had built a fake brick outer wall. There was now a small room between the fake wall and the real outer brick wall. The room was two and a half feet wide by about eight feet long. The new brick wall had been painted to look a hundred years old, paint peeling and waterstained. The original molding was put back. In front of the wall was a dilapidated wooden-backed bookcase. Under the lowest shelf was a sliding door.

"Keep a mattress in your secret room, along with water, hardtack and vitamins," said Mr. Smit as he left.

Corrie felt a chill. Would the Gestapo ever be in her room scratching the walls, sniffing about like loathsome rats? She must have faith in God. The Gestapo would never find the secret room. It was guarded by God's angels. Yes, in her own mind she would now call it the "angels' crib"!

With so many of their own men in uniform fighting the British in Africa, fighting the Russians in the east and occupying unfriendly countries all over Europe, the Germans desperately needed workers for their war factories. So in 1942 German soldiers began to raid Dutch homes. At any moment in any neighborhood German soldiers might appear in force to scour every house for Dutch men between the ages of sixteen and thirty. Then with rifles they nudged their captives into waiting trucks. The trucks took the men straight to Germany. To the Dutch it seemed a death sentence. Soon the Beje was refuge for young Dutch men too.

The hearts of the Dutch soared at the news crackling over the radio from England in January of 1943. The Russians had stopped the German advance eastward, and were even thought to be turning them back! The new year really seemed a turning point in the devil Hitler's fortunes. The British and Americans had routed the Germans from North Africa. At long last the sleeping giant America was fighting. If Hitler expected any help from his Japanese allies he would not get it. They were being pummeled by the Americans in the Pacific.

"Glory to God, there is hope for Holland at last," said Papa. "If we survive this winter."

That winter in Holland was so severe old Christoffels froze to death in his bed in a rooming house, the water in his wash basin frozen solid. Food and fuel were in short supply all winter. So were safe havens for Jews and young Dutchmen while the underground sought farms for them.

Even the few havens like the Beje were not safe. What happened at Mrs. De Boer's house just four blocks away from the Beje was an example of how everything could suddenly go wrong. Nineteen Jews were crowded into Mrs. De Boer's attic. In a wild impulse, eight of the young Jews took to the streets of Haarlem in the night. Before dawn all nineteen Jews and Mrs. De Boer herself had disappeared in the deadly clutches of the Gestapo.

Betsie was sad. "It could happen to us. We too have a good-sized operation."

Corrie shook her head. "And now we must get bigger."

Month after month the operation at Beje expanded. More and more Corrie became the command center. And more and more Dutch joined Corrie. It seemed that she always needed more messengers and more people with special skills. A fugitive would sicken and die, so Corrie needed a burial. A fugitive might become gravely ill, so Corrie needed a doctor immediately! She needed transportation for fugitives, identification papers for fugitives, food ration books for fugitives. Soon she had eighty people working directly in her operation!

Such a large distribution center for fleeing Jews and Dutch men got special treatment from the Dutch underground. The Beje's phone connection was restored. Buzzers were installed all through the house. Fugitives would scurry to the secret room once they sounded. Buttons which triggered the buzzers were hidden all over the lower part of the house. But those conveniences came with a heavy price.

"If the phone and alarm system are ever discovered by the Gestapo they have concrete evidence that we ten Booms are the worst of traitors to the glorious German Reich," worried Corrie.

"And the most loyal of the faithful to God's glory," countered Betsie.

After rising in the morning all who were in hiding had to drag their bedding, nightclothes and toilet articles up to the angels' crib. These were exchanged for their day things. Just before bed they exchanged their day things for their night things. They avoided using wastebaskets and ash trays. But these precautions were routine. The underground drilled them for the unexpected. The Gestapo liked to strike at mealtimes and in the middle of the night. In their mealtime drill all those in hiding at the Beje grabbed their dishes and huffed up the stairs. They practiced and practiced until they left nothing incriminating behind. The task was not made any easier by having constant additions to the household. Even with that, they slowly brought the time down: 90 seconds, 80 seconds, 70 seconds. . . .

They also drilled for night raids. Corrie hated that drill most of all. They did it after she was asleep. She knew those in hiding jumped up, turned their mattresses over so they were cold to the touch, then hustled their night things upstairs to the angels' crib. The part she despised was her part. They would shake her awake! "Where are you hiding the Jews?" they would scream in her face.

Corrie was a very heavy sleeper. Time and again she blurted something ruinous. It was a long time before she passed her part. How she dreaded the thought of a real raid in the night! Ironically, the fugitives made life in the Beje like old times in the evening. They sang. They studied the Bible. They played the pipe organ, the violin and the piano. They performed plays. They gave each other language lessons. Such were the ways they clung to their sanity in such mad times. And where was their deliverance? Where was the invasion of Europe? They had waited half of 1940 and all of 1941 and all of 1942 and most of 1943, hoping the British and Americans would come. Where were they? How long could the secret of the Beje last?

One day Corrie looked out the dining room window. Cowering in the alley was a woman, confusion and terror written all over her face.

"Katrien of all people!" Corrie rushed down and pulled her inside.

Katrien was babbling. "Your sister has gone crazy. . . ."

"Crazy? Nollie?"

"The Gestapo came to the house. And Nollie told them right out that Annaliese and I are Jews. I ran out the back door."

It was preposterous. But Corrie knew it was true. If the Gestapo asked Nollie a question she would tell them the truth. It was not long before the ten Booms learned Nollie was only a short distance away in the jail on Smedestraat. By all reports she was in high spirits, singing hymns. Poor Annaliese was in the old Jewish theater in Amsterdam, awaiting transport to Germany. Were there really death camps in Germany? That's what people were saying. It was monstrous, disgraceful, outrageous, intolerable, shameful, scandalous—in short, impossible. Yet for anyone who had suffered under Nazis it did not seem so impossible.

"Nollie can be so righteous!" sputtered Corrie. "How can I ever forgive her for how she doomed poor Annaliese?"

But six days later Corrie learned the underground had freed the Jews captive in Amsterdam. Annaliese was free! So the only harm done was to Nollie. Corrie felt terrible now for berating Nollie. And the news got worse. Nollie was transferred to federal prison in Amsterdam. Poor sweet

Nollie. But Corrie knew no prison could defeat Nollie's spirit. She was much too near God. Oh, how Nollie would frustrate her captors. How her sweet soprano would fill their cold-barred world with hymns.

But Corrie wasn't going to sit on her hands. She visited the doctor in charge of the prison hospital. And when she saw Doberman Pinschers in the waiting room she knew just what to say.

"How smart of you, doctor!" she said brightly in German. "You brought those lovely dogs with you to keep you company here in Holland."

"Do you like dogs?" He was suspicious but what dog-lover can resist talking about his incomparable dogs? Corrie breathlessly asked question after question about such excellent Dobermans. But the doctor finally tired of bragging and asked, "Why are you here?"

"My sister Nollie van Woerden is here." Corrie suddenly decided to be as recklessly honest as Nollie. "She's here for hiding a Jew. My sister has six children."

"I see." The doctor stood up. "You must go now."

Corrie went back to the Beje. Had she succeeded in anything at all? She busied herself again in her other dangerous activities but she was never too busy to stop and wonder. *Will Nollie be released? Is this the day?* She told herself to be patient. If the doctor was an ally to their cause she must not jeopardize such a valuable man by hanging around asking favors.

And not long afterwards, the ten Booms got an early Christmas present. Nollie was released from prison. The prison doctor said her blood pressure was dangerously low. Nollie shrugged. She never doubted God would take care of her. Her captivity had not gone to waste. She told all of them to pack a prison bag and keep it handy. Into

Corrie's went a Bible, a pencil, needle and thread, soap, toothbrush and comb.

"If you have any advance warning," cautioned Nollie, "dress in several sets of underwear and your warmest clothing."

In December the Beje started to celebrate not Christmas but Hanukkah. Betsie found a Hanukkah candlestand and each evening they performed the rituals. Their celebration was very authentic. And joyous. And loud. Corrie was chilled when the neighbor who lived next door asked discretely if they could sing with a little less volume. So their neighbors knew! Who else knew? Who walking by in the street might hear their Jewish festivities? How close was the Beje to discovery?

Each day seemed more treacherous than the last. And to compound the agony Corrie was now bed-ridden with the flu. She lay under her vaporizer, aching with every breath. Oh how she longed to hear the radio exultantly announce that the British and Americans were storming the shores of France! It was February of 1944. The Nazis had infested Holland for almost four years! How much longer could the amateurs in the Dutch underground hold out against ruthless snakes of the German Reich? How horrible Corrie felt. . . .

What was that sound? Thumping feet? Was she dreaming or was this real? Were those frantic whispers she heard? Had she heard the buzzer? She struggled to rise.

"Is this finally the end?" she mumbled groggily.

CHAPTER 6

Bodies were scrambling under her bookcase! "Yes!" blurted Corrie. "This nightmare is real!" The sliding door to the angels' crib slammed shut.

Voices came from below: harsh, demanding. In German. *"Schnell!"* Thumps. *"Passen sie auf!"* Nasty even for a German soldier. *"Wo sind die Juden?"* No, these weren't soldiers. The Gestapo!

In between the shrill barks below came a sound from the angels' crib. It was Mary, a seventy-six-year-old asthmatic, wheezing like a freight train!

"Oh please, Jesus, heal Mary. Now! I know you can do it," cried Corrie.

"Was ist das!" A man rushed into the bedroom. "Who are you talking to?" he barked in Dutch.

"No one you would know," mumbled Corrie as she clutched the covers around her.

"What did you say?" he growled.

"Why are you here?" asked Corrie, clutching the covers tighter.

"I ask the questions here!" The man wore a blue suit. He was tall but portly, with a pasty face. "What is your name?"

"Corrie ten Boom."

"Prove it."

She opened the pouch she wore around her neck. She pulled out her identification folder. "Here."

He yanked it from her hand and checked a notebook.

"So it is you!" He threw the folder back in her face.

"Why are you here?" She coughed at him with all her might.

"Cover your mouth! Have some decency." He backed up. "What is that smell? Menthol? Camphor? Get up at once and get out of here." He backed up through the door. "Your room smells like a sewer. You really are sick, aren't you?" His pasty face sagged with revulsion. "Come downstairs at once. And no funny business." He held a handkerchief over his nose and mouth. "This is such a dirty business at times," he complained to himself.

Corrie lurched to her feet. "Let me dress, please."

"Hurry up!"

She wanted to get out of the room as fast as possible. Mary might start wheezing any moment. She tugged clothes over her pajamas. She struggled to put on two sweaters.

"I said no funny business!" he barked.

"I have the chills," she said. She grabbed her winter coat. Where was her precious prison bag?

Her prison bag was by the sliding door!

How could she have been so careless? She couldn't draw attention to it now. What if Mary coughed or wheezed just then? Corrie had to keep coughing herself. The man might not notice an extra cough or wheeze. But how could she draw attention to the door? Yet how could she leave her precious bag? Prison would be hell without it. But she couldn't take the chance. She had to get out of her bedroom as soon as possible. The man was repelled by her room, yet now he seemed torn. He inched closer, as if he should really stay and poke around for a while. And what if Mary coughed? Corrie lurched out of the room without the bag—and stumbled down the stairs.

"Be careful," said the man. "Cover your mouth."

A soldier stood in front of one of the second floor bedrooms. Hadn't there been a prayer meeting there earlier? It was Willem's meeting. It was real. Even Nollie and her son Peter were usually in his prayer meetings. It gave them an excuse to keep coming to the Beje. Oh surely they were all gone by now. What time was it? How long had she slept? What day was it?

In the dining room a man in a brown suit sat at the table. Corrie cried, "Papa. Betsie. Toos." They were sitting on chairs against the wall. Daylight streamed through the dining room window.

The pasty-faced man in the blue suit said in German, "I've got Corrie ten Boom here." He paused for effect. "The ringleader."

"Ringleader?" the man at the table answered in German. He looked up. He had been counting silver coins that had been hidden under the staircase with the radio. "That old frump?" He shrugged. "Take her downstairs and find out where the Jews are hidden." He shivered and glanced toward the barren coal hearth. It rarely had a fire these days. "You people live like barbarians. I'm surprised you have chairs." He began counting again.

The man in the blue suit prodded Corrie through the work room into the front showroom. He slapped her hard. "Attention now!"

She held her stinging face. "What do you want?"

"Where are you hiding the Jews?"

"We have none."

He slapped her again. "Where are the stolen ration books?"

"We don't have any."

He slapped her again. "Where are you hiding the Jews?"

"Oh please, Jesus, stop him." She was coughing. She tasted blood in her mouth.

He lowered his arm and backed up. "What do you have? It's not tuberculosis, is it? What a dirty business this is." He scowled at his notebook again. "Which one is Betsie?"

Minutes later Corrie sat in Betsie's chair in the dining room and Betsie was in the showroom taking the blows from the man in the blue suit. But soon she was back, slender and limp, lips trembly and swollen. Corrie rose and helped sit her down.

Betsie whispered, "I feel sorry for that man."

A woman blundered in the alley door. "I heard they arrested—"

"Quiet!" screamed Corrie.

"You be quiet!" The man in the blue suit struck Corrie.

The man at the table glared at her. "We might have learned something from that silly fool," he said to the other man in German. "Bring her up here."

But the woman froze. Now she knew she was in the hands of the Gestapo. Corrie was depressed. So they were arresting others too. And there sat aged Papa. *Please, Lord Jesus, don't let them hurt Papa.* She heard noises of splintering wood above them. Had they found the angels' crib? But there were no screams. No cries of triumph. Perhaps not.

So far the Gestapo had found the hidden silver which was supposed to have been surrendered to the Nazis long ago. They found the radio, the telephone, even the alarm system. Only a fool would have not realized the ten Booms were in very deep trouble. There would be no evading Nazi injustice for these violations.

A man blundered in the alley door. He was arrested.

Then another man. Finally the traffic stopped. The word was out. The Beje had been raided.

The man at the table stood up. "I guess we can leave now," he said in Dutch. He smiled evilly at Corrie. "Aren't you happy? Your Jewish roaches are safe, aren't they? Well, when you are rotting in prison, reflect on this. We will surround your house for as long as it takes. The Jewish roaches in your secret room will turn into mummies. It will be a very long, a very painful death!"

But Corrie was happy. *Trust God*, she reminded herself. There was still hope for the people in the angels' crib. The Gestapo had not found them. The Gestapo had failed!

Suddenly captives began filing out of the second floor bedroom, past the dining room and down the stairs. There was Nollie! And Peter! And Willem! Every ten Boom, it seemed. Thank God Mama had not lived to see this awful day.

Inside the police station, not police but soldiers herded them down a corridor into a gymnasium. Thirty-five people had been arrested at the Beje. The men of the Gestapo looked very proud. This was quite a roundup for them—so large, they would probably brag that they needed a gymnasium to hold all the criminals. Would the two men in suits be thinking of promotions? What normal person could know what went through such sick Nazi minds?

In the gymnasium the captives were allowed to talk among themselves. They even used the toilets off the gymnasium to flush papers that should not be discovered. So the Gestapo was not so smart after all—just active and evil. That night ended just as almost every night of Corrie's life ended. In a deep steady voice Papa delivered the word of God. This night he read Psalm 91. Yes, how

"He is my refuge and my fortress, my God, in whom I trust," repeated Corrie to herself.

The next morning they were marched out of the police station. In the street waited a long green bus. Some soldiers were already inside it. Corrie squeezed onto one double seat with Papa and Betsie. The bus rumbled across the town square. Farther back in the crowded bus were Nollie and Willem and Peter. And Toos. Everyone of them wanted to get off but couldn't. Corrie remembered her vision the night of the Nazi invasion. They were being taken away against their will in a wagon drawn by enormous black horses. Now she knew what it meant. Her vision of May 10, 1940 had come true February 29, 1944.

"February 29," whispered Betsie to Corrie, "is good. It's one anniversary I don't want to have every year."

It was a bright winter day. The bus headed not east to Amsterdam but south along the dunes that held back the North Sea. In two hours the bus was rumbling through the streets of The Hague. They stopped in front of a building. In Dutch Willem told them this was the Gestapo head-quarters for all of Holland. Inside the headquarters was not terror, but grinding bureaucracy. Clerks behind a high counter asked questions and typed answers onto papers. One answer was never enough. Every question had to be asked a dozen times—not as a shrewd tool of interrogation but the result of an over-reaching fumbling bureaucracy. Was this the true hell behind the Nazis? Were they a col-lection of cold-blooded petty clerks? If Corrie had not been so sick with the flu she probably would have laughed. How could anyone respect such fools?

There was a fuss when Papa reached the front of the line. "We don't want old codgers like him in our system," growled the head man in German. "Let someone else take care of him." He leaned over to Papa. He shouted in Dutch, "Listen up, old man. If I send you home will you behave yourself?"

"If I go home," said Papa firmly, "I will open my door again to anyone who knocks."

The head man's face reddened. In German he barked, "Type this fool's papers!"

"It is an honor to go to prison for God's people," persisted Papa. "I pity you."

Many hours later soldiers prodded them into the back of a canvas-topped army truck. They bounced and rattled on a long ride. But too soon they stopped. Where were they? Corrie could see nothing. Willem told them they were inside the federal prison in Scheveningen. They scrambled down out of the truck to stand dazed in a courtyard surrounded by high brick walls. Soldiers prodded them inside a long low building. They lined up facing a wall inches from their noses.

"Women prisoners, follow me!" screamed a woman's voice.

Corrie turned. Where was Papa? There he was, not far away. "Good-bye, Papa. God be with you," she cried.

"God be with you, Papa," echoed Betsie.

"And God goes with you, my daughters," Papa said in a voice that was clear but thin with exhaustion.

A soldier approached with a rifle. They must keep moving. Corrie held Betsie's hand and rushed ahead with the flow of prisoners. Where was Nollie? Then she saw Nollie just ahead. A door banged behind them. Coconut-palm matting ran down the center of the hallway. It sponged under her tired legs. The prisoners were urged along by women guards now, armed with billy clubs.

"Follow the matron—but keep off the mat!" barked a

guard. "Prisoners never walk on the mats."

The flow in the hallway stopped. They waited their turn to surrender everything of value to a woman at a desk. Corrie gave up her Alpina wristwatch, a gold ring and a few Dutch guilders. Her belongings disappeared into a large envelope. Then they marched down a cold hallway scarred by narrow metal doors, stopping only for their captors to unlock a door and roughly shove one of the women inside. Betsie was the first sister to go into a cell. Nollie went in a cell two doors beyond Betsie's cell. If only Corrie were next. She would at least be close to her dear sisters.

But they went on and on, turned a corner, turned another corner and yet another, until Corrie was hopelessly disoriented.

CHAPTER 7

Finally a guard sent Corrie stumbling inside a cell. Four women were already in the cell. Three thin mats were on the floor beside one cot.

The matron snapped, "Give this prisoner the cot."

Corrie began coughing. The air was clammy.

"Don't put a sick woman in with us," whined one of the inmates.

Corrie collapsed on the cot, clutching her coat around her aching body.

Later a hand struck her. "Wake up. It's food call," said a voice.

Corrie sat up. A square of metal dropped down in the door, forming a shelf. Four tin plates heaped with steaming gruel were placed there.

"We get an extra portion," screamed one of the inmates. "We have a new one in here!"

Corrie looked away from the watery porridge. "I can't eat now." And she collapsed again. The grumbling subsided as the four divided up her portion. When they finished they put the five plates back on the food shelf.

It didn't take long to learn prison routine. Once a day they got hot food, usually gruel. Once a day they got a piece of dark bread. Once a day they passed out the bucket they had to use for a toilet. It was returned empty. Once a day they passed out the wash basin full of gray water. It was returned with clean water.

All day long one of the women walked the length of the narrow cell. Six steps from end to end. One naked light bulb burned overhead. There were no windows.

In spite of her illness Corrie tried to talk to the women. They were curt. They guarded their pasts. Their universe now was prison. It was too painful to speak of the outside. Would Corrie get that way?

A noise rattled in the hall. Feet padded in the hall too. "That's a trustee with the medical cart. Someone is sick," said one woman.

A door opened. There were footsteps.

"That's the matron," said the same woman. "I'll bet she found someone with an extra blanket."

A door opened and closed somewhere in the hall. There were footsteps.

"That's someone in Cell 316 being lead away by a guard. Toward the interior. For a hearing," said the same woman.

"How can you know all that?" asked Corrie, unbelieving.

"She's been here three years," snarled one of the other cellmates bitterly.

Three years! Corrie found that fact so depressing she shut up. A hunted animal didn't have senses finer-tuned than the woman who had been here three years. She knew every sound. How the woman must have longed for freedom. Or had she given up? It seemed useless to ask.

Corrie thought about Papa. How would her dear Papa survive this cold, miserable place? He was eighty-four. She always felt he lived on because he was buoyed up by love and friendship in the Beje. How would he do now?

Boredom became a challenge. One of the women

played solitaire all day. The ten Booms had never played cards. But Corrie gave it a try. Solitaire was fun. But she began to use the game like a ouija board. If the cards were good, that meant good news was coming. If the cards were bad, that meant nothing at all was going to happen. After a while the card game seemed so devilish she had to stop playing. And she wasn't getting her health back. As often as not she was limp as a rag on the cot, coughing and aching.

One day in her second week of imprisonment the matron unlocked the door. "Get your hat and coat, ten Boom!"

"Something unusual is up!" blurted the inmate who had been there three years. Her mouth was gaping.

"Good or bad?" asked Corrie.

"Shut up, prisoner!" growled the matron. "Come with me."

What was it? Was something waiting for Corrie too horrible to imagine?

Corrie would not allow herself to think the worst. "Are you freeing me?" she asked.

"Shut up, prisoner!"

Oh God, if freedom is your will, please let it be true. How Corrie hated the cell. And using the bucket in front of others was so degrading. And why couldn't she be free? Nollie had been freed from a federal prison after admitting she hid a Jew. Oh, it was wonderful to be out of the cell. She refused to think about the worst possibility.

"Stay off the mat!" barked the matron.

Corrie felt better as she stepped out into the courtyard with the high brick walls. She gazed at the marvelous blue sky. Her outing was to a doctor. After he had taken her temperature and listened to her chest with his stethoscope, he diagnosed pleurisy. A nurse pressed something into her hand. It was wrapped in paper. Corrie shoved it into her coat pocket.

"You're back!" exclaimed the woman whose hearing had been acutely tuned for three years. "Where did you go?"

"A medical clinic." Corrie waited to hear the door lock and footsteps retreat down the hallway. Then she pulled out the bundle. "I have something." She unwrapped it. "Soap!" She held up two bars. "Who wants to wash first?" The soap was snatched out of her hand. She held up a packet. "Look, safety pins."

"What treasure," said one of the inmates.

"Finally, the best of all," said Corrie. "The Gospels." She held up four tiny books.

The others drew back. "Are you crazy? If you get caught. . ."

"*Kalte kost* for that too?" asked Corrie in a tired voice. It seemed every infraction in prison was punished by *kalte kost*, which meant only cold food was given to the prisoner. And that meant only bread, no hot gruel as bad as it was.

"Much worse," said the one who had been there three years. "If you're caught with a Bible the Nazis double your sentence!"

That punishment took Corrie's breath away. "How the Nazis fear God's Word!"

And just two days later the matron entered again. "Get your hat and coat, ten Boom!"

"Something's up again," said the astonished inmate who had been there three years.

"Stay off the mat!" snapped the matron in the hallway. Had a cellmate squealed on Corrie? Surely there was no reason to call her out of the cell again. But the matron finally stopped and unlocked the door of a cell.

"Get inside."

Corrie entered an empty cell. The door slammed behind her. The cot smelled foul. Yes, someone had vomited on it. The stench seemed to trigger something—for she became very sick, even feverish. She collapsed on the stinking cot and couldn't even get up to get her food when later it came through the slot in the door.

She cried to the retreating footsteps, "Did the doctor tell you I am dying? Is that why you isolated me?"

The second time they brought food a hand hurled a hunk of bread toward the cot. Next, a medical trustee visited her. He gave her a dose of medicine that tasted as foul as it looked, then took her temperature. All of the menial work was done by trustees. She asked the trustee about Papa. But the trustee would not talk. A trustee was not about to jeopardize his privileged position, whatever that got him. Corrie was sure she would never be a trustee.

After a while the medical trustee stopped coming. And Corrie began to feel better, even though this cell was much colder than the other cell. And why not? There was a barred window high above her, open to the outside. Oh, what if Papa had been locked in such a cell? The month of March had been bitterly cold. It was now April. She had been in prison one month.

She had never reflected much on weather. It was hard to imagine a country that had weather easier to predict than Holland's. From midnight to afternoon the temperature ranged a mere ten degrees. Along the coast in places like Haarlem and here at Scheveningen many days were sunny. In the hottest part of summer the temperature hit a maximum of about 70 degrees during the day and dropped to 60 at night. In the coldest blast of winter the temperature dropped just to freezing at night and rose to about 40 during the day. Corrie had been lucky. During the very coldest weather she had been in an interior cell. If she had been in this cell the first week she would have died.

"Praise God," she said to the blue sky through the barred window, "for fair weather."

As the weather improved the window became an ally. For one hour a day, a ray of sunshine swept the lower reaches of the cell. Corrie bathed in its glory. It made her feel healthy again. But health brought memories back. Worry over Papa crushed her. What had happened to all her cohorts in the underground? And what about the fugitives in the angels' crib?

She had neglected her precious Gospels. Her eyes had been too bad to read. Praise God Papa had encouraged her to memorize verses. That satisfied her hunger for the Bible. Now she was well enough to read again. She read constantly. The Gospels rejuvenated her more than the sunshine. How could she have sunk so low as to doubt and brood? What seemed like failure could be a colossal success yet. Her spirits rose.

Her birthday came. "Fifty-two today," she said to no one but herself.

She got a treat two days later on April 17: her first shower in six weeks. She was feeling much better. How had she survived? Praise God. Life seemed to spring from God's grace now. An ant scurried out of a crack in the floor of her cell. It was a major event. Corrie felt honored. It had seemed for a while no life was so low as to visit such a cell as hers. But now she had an ant visiting, a forerunner of better things. She scattered bread crumbs by the crack. She must make sure her visitor returned. And it did. She now had three wonderful gifts: the sunshine, the ant and the Gospels.

Then she received a package! Nothing was written on it but Corrie's name and the address of the prison, but Corrie knew it was from Nollie's family, the van Woerdens. In it were sandwiches, a brown cake and a pan of porridge. And there was more: a needle and thread, two bottles of vitamins and a brilliant red towel! How Nollie's family understood prisons now.

"Inmates in this gray hell crave color," she told the ant.

The evening of April 20 was very unusual. For seven weeks the prison had been like a tomb. Usually she had to strain to hear nothing more than padding feet and squeaking cart wheels. But this evening she heard shouts. Yes, shouts. What was it? She was very blessed. The food shelf in her door had been left open. She pressed her ear against the opening.

"What is going on?" shouted someone. "Where are the guards? Are we being rescued? Are the British and Americans here at last?"

"You might as well hope for a visit from the Queen," answered a voice choked with bitterness. "It's Hitler's birthday. The guards are celebrating with the other miserable Nazis."

"Don't waste this time complaining," urged another voice. "We can exchange information."

What happened next was miraculous. Somehow these poor lost souls organized and disciplined themselves to spread news all around the prison. Messages flew back and forth. It was a glorious time. Corrie learned Nollie was released! *Oh Nollie. Wouldn't you know it? Nollie always landed on her feet like a cat!* Her son Peter was released too. Praise God for that. And Willem. Praise the Lord. And

Toos. The news stunned Corrie. Had they all been released? *Please God, let it be true.* Then she heard Betsie was still in prison. And no one knew anything at all about Caspar ten Boom.

"Where is Papa?"

One week later another package was thrown into her cell. Corrie recognized Nollie's handwriting! Inside was Nollie's favorite sweater of pale blue with flowers embroidered over the pocket. How wonderful! And more vitamins. And cookies. Rewrapping her treasures Corrie noticed something odd about Nollie's handwriting. It seemed slanted toward the stamp. Quickly she worked the stamp loose with water. Yes! There was a message under the stamp!

"All the watches in your closet are safe," read Corrie in a whisper.

So the fugitives in the angels' crib in the Beje had escaped! Praise God. Corrie should not have worried so much about them after being processed by the Gestapo in The Hague. Such bunglers could not sustain a watch around the Beje week after week. Constant vigil was nothing but an empty threat by the Gestapo, hoping she would panic and talk.

She had only one worry now: Papa. "Where is he?"

One day Corrie was pulling thread from the red towel to embroider colorful figures on the very pajamas she wore the day she was arrested. Her food shelf opened and a letter drifted in like a beautiful snowflake. It was from Nollie!

The words were crushing. "No! Not that—"

CHAPTER 8

"**P**apa is dead!"

Must she read more? How she dreaded to read the next lines. But she must. *Trust God,* she reminded herself. She could wait one month, dying every second, and the letter would still have to be read. She read how he died after only nine days. The letter informed her that Betsie knew about it too.

"How I would like to talk to Betsie now," sobbed Corrie. "Poor Papa."

No, Corrie mustn't grieve in the wrong way. Not with pity or sorrow. She must be sorry only because she missed his wonderful presence. Papa said he would gladly die for the Jews. And he did. Then she realized Papa was now with Mama too. And dear Aunt Anna. And feisty Aunt Jans. And Aunt Bep. And Papa's father Willem. And Papa's mother. And his grandfather Gerrit. What glory. How she wanted to see them too. Was dying so bad? But she remembered Paul's letter to Philippi. Now matter how tempting it was to end our trials on earth, it was pure selfishness.

"I must fight the good fight for the furtherance and joy of faith on earth first," she reminded herself.

One day Corrie was allowed to exercise in an open area inside the prison. Corrie could smell the North Sea beyond the wall. Her rubbery legs walked a rectangular path around a lawn. Other prisoners walked there too. Shrubs by the path flowered red. Primroses were in bloom. The sun was warm. The sky was blue. Was this so bad? Surely she could endure this. Did monsters keep such gardens as this?

But then she saw a freshly dug trench. No. She must not even think her suspicions. But it spoiled her reverie. She noticed now the high walls were topped with broken glass. There was a burning smell in the air too. It smelled like nothing she had ever smelled before. Her soul wanted to cry out. Another inmate walked by her and whispered the stench was from burning flesh. The prison has a crematorium. *No! That is too preposterous,* thought Corrie. *Not even Nazis are that evil.* Suddenly her ears were pounded by noises beyond the walls. *Is that a jackhammer?* She was afraid to look at the other inmate.

"That was a machine gun," whispered the inmate, "I know. . . ."

Corrie welcomed her gray cell. *Oh Lord, let me out only when I can walk with children of the Light.* It was only days later that Corrie listened to rain fall outside her window. It was a gray day when one wanted nothing to happen. What good could happen on such a gloomy day? She chided herself. She heard the footsteps of a guard. *Just keep right on walking,* prayed Corrie.

She heard a key in the lock. The door opened and a woman guard stepped inside. "Come with me, ten Boom."

Corrie asked, "Do I need my coat and hat?"

"No!" The guard raised her billy club. "Do as I say! Come with me. Stay off the mat!"

The guard led Corrie into a courtyard somewhere in the midst of the prison. In the courtyard were four small huts. The guard knocked on the door of one hut. Corrie stood beside her, rain dripping down her face. After a voice inside answered, the guard pushed Corrie in the door. There stood a tall thin man in the crisp gray and black uniform of the Nazis.

"I'm Lieutenant Rahms," he said in Dutch. "Sit down. It's chilly in here," he added, more to himself than Corrie.

Corrie sat. The chair had a back and arms. She felt so privileged. She watched the Lieutenant scoop coal into a small potbellied stove. He was in no hurry. She enjoyed every minute of the experience. Did he know that? Was that why he dawdled, stirring the coals around with a poker? How could she credit a Nazi with such compassion? But soon he had a cozy fire started. She smelled and felt the warmth. What luxury.

He sat down. "If I'm going to help you, you must tell me everything."

So that was it. The snake was just getting her to relax. "What would you like to know?" she asked dully.

Lieutenant Rahms discretely probed. His face was chiseled with sharp features, a face easy to interpret as evil. Yet the face had something soft and haunting too. Corrie had seen that look before. But she must not jump to conclusions with a Nazi. After many questions Corrie figured out what he was after. He seemed to think the Beje might have been a center for planning raids on food offices and stealing food ration books. Corrie relaxed, blissful in her ignorance. She could betray no one in any operations that raided food offices. She had long been out of that business.

"I don't know what you mean," she kept repeating.

All the while she enumerated her many activities before the occupation. Yes, she took teenaged girls hiking and camping. Yes, she helped raise children left in Holland by missionaries. Yes, she gave Sunday school lessons to retarded children. . . .

Finally the Lieutenant sighed. "I believe we have talked enough." He looked at his notepad. He had written nothing but doodles. He rose and opened the door. "Guard, take the prisoner back to her cell."

Next day Corrie was back. This time the Lieutenant held their conference in the courtyard. They sat by a wall. "You need sun," he said. During a long pause Corrie closed her eyes and reveled in the sun. Finally he said, "I couldn't sleep last night. I kept thinking about the work I do. And I kept thinking about the work you used to do before we Germans came here to Holland."

This time she was sure about the look in his face. Corrie had not counseled hundreds of young people out of despair without knowing all the symptoms of someone truly crying out for God. "You are in darkness, Lieutenant."

"A good person like you can not know darkness like mine. . . ."

"Jesus is the light of the world. Whoever follows Jesus will never walk in darkness. . . ."

Corrie told him the story of her life. He couldn't believe such a righteous family existed. He asked again and again to hear about Papa and Mama and Aunt Jans and Aunt Anna. His curiosity was insatiable. Finally she knew he believed her.

"If only I could raise my own family in Bremen that way," he lamented.

"There is always a second chance with Jesus. It's never too late."

She had four hearings with the Lieutenant. In one session when the Lieutenant's hut had not the slightest chill he stoked up a fire in the small stove. Then he took a file folder from his desk and stood by the stove. Corrie could see it was her file. Her file thinned to almost nothing as paper after paper disappeared in flames.

"I believe we are warm enough now," he said. "I have a paper for you to sign. It's a deposition summarizing your knowledge of the Dutch underground. I have seldom met a person more ignorant of the underground than you."

The first week in June she was escorted to the Lieutenant's office again. Inside was Betsie! And Nollie! And Willem! In tears, she hugged them. The Lieutenant excused himself so they could talk privately. He looked haggard and haunted.

When the door closed Corrie cried, "We are being released!"

"No, it's the reading of Papa's will."

Willem said, "But time is on our side. Everyone thinks the invasion is coming! Pray to God that the British and Americans will soon head this way. The Russians are already rolling over the Germans from the other direction. Praise God the Nazis are almost finished."

While they talked Nollie pressed a pouch into Corrie's hand. It contained a complete Bible! Corrie quickly put the string of the pouch over her head and slipped the treasure down inside her dress. Suddenly the Lieutenant returned to read the will. He had left them alone as long as he could. The will surprised no one. There was no money, only the Beje. And Papa left it to shelter Corrie and Betsie as long as they wished.

Willem prayed, "Lord Jesus, we thank You for bringing us together for a while. Take this good man, Lieutenant Rahms, and his family into Your constant care. Amen." The Lieutenant's face came alive with hope.

The prison erupted a few days later. Guards screamed at the inmates to throw their few belongings into pillow slips and stand at attention in the hallways. Then they were herded outside. In the courtyard were buses! Corrie searched desperately for Betsie. Maybe they could get together at last. But Betsie was nowhere to be seen among the milling prisoners. *Oh please Jesus, let us be together again,* prayed Corrie, as the buses spewed black smoke and churned across the countryside.

After the buses unloaded them at the railway station they streamed onto railroad cars. Corrie hung back. Where was Betsie? *Oh please God, let us be together.* As she was jostled along toward a railroad car she saw Betsie behind her. Her prayer was answered! She waited and threw her arms around her. They were giddy as they found seats together on the car. How she missed Betsie. Oh how Betsie could make any suffering joyous.

"The British and Americans must be on their way," said Betsie.

"Is that why we are being moved?" Corrie shook her head. "And still the Nazis worry about small fry like us. Praise the Lord the devils are such fools."

"Thank the Lord we Dutch do not have such an evil government," said Betsie. "You know, Corrie, many Germans are victims of the Nazi madness too." And they both prayed for the Lieutenant and his family.

"We must try to stay together no matter what," said Corrie.

"Praise God that we are not going east to Germany," whispered Betsie at one point. "I thought I saw in the distance the cathedral in Delft."

"If you're right, we're going south."

Corrie was so happy to be with Betsie she had not worried where they were headed. Betsie didn't really worry at all. Betsie was certain every action was planned by God, no matter how hard it was for a human mind to accept. But Corrie wasn't at all sure of that. Now she was worried.

Before she went to prison she really did not believe the terrible stories about death camps in Germany. But how could she doubt the stories now? The wheels changed pitch. The train was zipping across a trestle. The trestle went on and on. Only one bridge was that wide. The bridge at Moerdijk.

She turned to Betsie. "We're headed. . ."

"South," said Betsie calmly. "Not east to Germany."

They hugged each other and thanked God.

Sometime in the night they stopped. They were rudely prodded off the train. Soldiers brandishing rifles bordered a rough path through the woods. In the blackness the prisoners slogged through puddles where it had rained. A soldier brutally kicked a woman who wandered off the path. Corrie and Betsie winced and struggled on. *Oh, how malleable people are,* thought Corrie. *We prisoners have no idea how long this nightmare will continue, yet we labor on obediently, almost complacent, no reward except that we avoid as much abuse as possible and remain alive.*

They learned they were still in Holland on the perimeter of a prison camp near the village of Vught. This was not a Dutch prison. It was a concentration camp built by the Nazis for political prisoners. That fact was enough to alert everyone that this camp might not be an improvement over Scheveningen. For days the newcomers were idle as they were being processed into the camp.

"It seems the Nazis were not quite prepared for all the inconveniences of an invasion," said one newcomer bitterly.

One day Corrie and Betsie were prodded into a long line. The news filtered back down the line: twenty women at a time were being herded into a shower. Finally as the two sisters neared the head of the line they heard a guard shout, "Undress!" His voice was nasty, but there was more in it. Soon they could see the men guards relishing their power, laughing as they enjoyed the sight of naked women wiggling under the icy water. The women had to shower right out in the open!

"Oh please God," prayed Corrie, "don't let this abomination happen to sweet innocent Betsie."

CHAPTER 9

Moments before their group of twenty was to undress, a guard yelled, "We are out of uniforms. Send the cows back later." His voice was bored. How much flesh can even corrupt Nazi eyes absorb?

When the women's camp received a new supply of uniforms, the men guards had returned to the men's camp. Corrie and Betsie showered under the eyes of women guards, nasty enough but still a small miracle.

"Praise the Lord," said Betsie.

In their barracks lived 150 women. The inmates slept on real beds with two blankets. There was an undercurrent of joy. Camp life really was better than prison life. The British and Americans were coming. It was inevitable now. The prisoners were sure. Corrie didn't even mind wearing a uniform of blue overalls with a red stripe down each leg. Her own clothes had rotted after three months of constant wear. But the crude wooden clogs they were forced to clomp around in were painful.

"Line up, prisoners!" ordered a prisoner.

He was an *oberkapo,* or "boss." The Nazis were short of soldiers. Work was largely in the hands of prisoners. As icy-veined as any Nazi, the *oberkapo* examined the newcomers. How power corrupts. The *oberkapo* contemptuously shunted frail Betsie aside into a group of the infirm who sewed prison uniforms. Corrie was marched to the "Phillips factory," which was no more than an additional barracks situated between the women's camp and the men's camp. Hundreds of men and women prisoners sat on benches hunched over radio parts on long tables. Guards rarely strolled the aisles. The work was supervised by another *oberkapo*, a soft-spoken, very shrewd Dutchman named Moorman.

He soothed even the Nazis. "We can increase production substantially, Captain," he would say in the monotone of a good colorless engineer, "at no sacrifice to quality."

But as soon as the Nazis were gone, the barracks exploded with laughter. After grim Scheveningen Corrie couldn't believe such high spirits. Was this one of the notorious Nazi work camps? It was hot in the barracks in summer. Corrie rolled up her pant legs. A girl suddenly flung a mug of water on Moorman. He retaliated. Tables were soaked. No one cared. Soon others carried both of the water-throwers into the bathroom. The girl was held in a large industrial sink, squirming and laughing under the gushing faucets.

"This is quite an unusual 'factory'," said Corrie.

With Corrie's watchmaking dexterity she was soon assembling radios instead of sorting parts as they arrived. The real art was to assemble the radio in such a way that it was hopelessly defective but not obviously defective. The radios were installed in German fighter planes. More than once Corrie woke from a nightmare in which a German pilot was screaming into a dead radio that a fellow pilot had a Spitfire on his tail, just before the Messerschmidt was blasted out of the sky! She didn't tell Betsie what she was doing. Oh, how the Nazis corrupted!

The undermanned Nazis did reward the workers for their twelve-hour work day. Here at Vught they ate three times a day. And the food was better than the food at Scheveningen. After lunch the workers even had an hour off to rest. It was summer, so Corrie would stretch out on the ground for a nap. There was plenty of time for chatter while they worked—if no guards were strolling the aisles.

One day a voice woke her. "Corrie?"

Corrie blinked the sleep out of her eyes. "Mien? What joy!"

Mien van Dantzig—the very sister of Hennie who had worked in the watch shop in the Beje—also worked in the Phillips factory. Mien was a thin young woman and very sly. Corrie soon learned she was a "scrounger." She helped the nurse in the camp. If a prisoner needed medicine—or just about anything else—Mien might be able to get it for her.

Talk in the camp transcended gossip. To survive, one listened to information, judged its credibility and shared it with others. She and Betsie even found out the name of their betrayer! He was a Dutchman from Ermelo. How Corrie hated him. Yet, Jesus commanded her to forgive enemies. But how could she ever forgive the wretch who caused Papa to die? And to think what suffering she and Betsie had been through. Betsie was weaker every day. Yet Betsie had forgiven the traitor, even prayed for him!

One night she argued about it with Betsie. "Pray for that devil? Never!" said Corrie.

"Think how much he must hate himself," answered Betsie. "Think how much he is suffering."

Corrie was skeptical but Betsie prevailed. Corrie forced herself to pray for him too. She knew from years of trying to live in Christ that a righteous act, no matter how reluctantly performed, often captured the heart. But she doubted it would work in the case of this dreadful traitor. However, praying did do something for her. For the first time since she learned the man's identity, Corrie fell asleep without bitterness and anger.

Prison routine rarely varied. Inmates stumbled out for first roll call at five o'clock. At five-thirty they ate black bread and drank weak coffee. Then Corrie hiked to the Phillips factory where she worked until six o'clock that evening. She trudged back to spend precious free time with Betsie. She kept telling herself that a Christian can never really be imprisoned.

They were allowed to exchange letters again with Nollie's family and Willem's family. Corrie could scarcely believe her eyes when she opened Nollie's first letter.

"Lieutenant Rahms phoned Nollie to say that the letter which would set us free had been sent!" Corrie told Betsie.

"Hallelujah! Freedom!"

Was it possible? Corrie and Betsie were breathless as they motioned a gnarled veteran named Floor to meet them in the latrine. All important business took place in the latrine. The men guards, as brutal as they were, never went there. A lookout was posted to watch out for the women guards.

The veteran Floor told the sisters, "If you helped Jews that gets you locked up for six months."

"Are you sure?" asked Corrie.

"You know the Germans. If that is what it says in their little Nazi rule book that is what it is. You'd have to get that crackpot Hitler to change one of his own rules."

"Six months?" cried Corrie. "Let me see. We started our sentence the last day of February. March, April, May, June, July, August. We'll be free by September 1!"

Corrie and Betsie rejoiced. Less than two months to go! They could serve that time easily. They gave Bible lessons to others. They sang hymns. They gave evening devotions. As more time passed they began to give sermons. Several dozen inmates, putting their bitterness on hold, listened to the sisters deliver the Gospel.

Corrie had gained twenty pounds in the camp! She could almost have become complacent if Betsie hadn't worried her so. Poor Betsie weighed less than one hundred pounds. Her glasses were always broken, always askew. She had to pin her overall straps closer together to keep her modesty. Even packages from Nollie crammed with sausages and fudge couldn't keep Betsie from wasting away. And Corrie discovered the sewing brigade was no picnic. Many times the brigade had to braid rope, and at the end of the day Betsie's long delicate hands were raw and bleeding. If there was one thing an anemic person couldn't withstand very long it was bleeding.

The noises coming from the men's camp next to the women's camp squelched the last crumb of complacency Corrie might have harbored. Every rifle shot ringing from the men's camp brought suspicions of an execution. At first Betsie refused to believe executions were so routine. It was too monstrous. But Corrie worked at the Phillips factory with men from the camp next to theirs.

"Executions are not just rumors," Corrie told her reluctantly. "They are real."

How Corrie longed for September 1 and freedom! Miracles did happen in the camp. Betsie was inmate number 1130 and Corrie 1131. One morning at roll call when the cold-blooded matron called someone who was to be released, her voice choked. She gasped, "Inmate number one!"

The very first woman inmate of the camp lurched forward from the ranks. As the others marched off to work the poor ghost of a woman slumped on a bench. How many years had she been there? What "crime" had she many years had she been there? What "crime" had she committed against the glorious German Reich? Praise to God she was free at last.

And then came a delicious rumor: the British and Americans had taken Paris back! Their ground forces were knifing through France. They would soon cut Hitler's throat! Could it be true? Soon they saw proof with their own eyes. Almost daily by the end of August hundreds of silvery planes glimmered overhead, all headed east into Germany. One afternoon after the great silvery armada passed overhead the women heard what must have been a tremendous battle in the sky just east of them. They laughed like fools as projectiles snicked trees around them and pinged into the barracks. Five women were hospitalized, injured by shrapnel.

Days later, explosions rocked the area.

"Bombs?" asked Corrie at the Phillips factory.

"No," said Moorman, "The Nazis are blowing up all the bridges." He had never been so serious. Oh, he was a wonderful actor around the Nazis. But something else was in his face. A deep worry.

"What do you suppose it is?" Corrie asked Betsie later.

"I don't know. Let's find Floor."

Floor turned their blood to ice. "These Nazis are going to pull out and blow up every bridge between here and Germany. The question is: What are they going to do with us? Take us with them? Or leave us here? And if they do leave us here, is it with a song of freedom on our lips—or rotting in a mass grave. Which do you think Nazis will do?" She sounded very bitter.

"Surely they won't execute the whole camp?" said Betsie in horror.

"Maybe not us. They don't respect us. They think we

are weaklings. But I'm not so sure about the men."

Corrie was stunned. For hundreds of reasons. She could only say, "But our time is almost up."

Floor laughed sourly. "Do you think they're going to process anyone for release now?" And she continued as if speaking just to herself, "Winter is a very bad time in the camps. And this winter will be the worst yet. No fuel. Little food. The weak ones will never. . ." She seemed to notice Betsie. "Never mind. Enough of this doomsday bilge."

Corrie said unconvincingly, "She's wrong, Betsie. We'll be free on September 1."

As the magic date approached, conditions worsened. Executions in the men's camp were more frequent. Guards were extremely edgy in the women's camp. The women guards even got ugly with the prostitutes, who were usually immune to any kind of punishment. The prostitutes were protected by the men guards. The women guards despised the prostitutes but feared the men guards more. As a result the prostitutes strolled out of the barracks late to roll call, violated the boundaries of the camp, lolled about, and sassed any woman guard any time they felt like it. But now they were being harassed by the women guards. That new attitude frightened the other women. It didn't take a genius to figure out that the women guards knew the exalted status of the prostitutes was about to end. And that was not good news for any of the prisoners.

Finally the long awaited day arrived: September 1!

CHAPTER 10

September 1 was a Friday.

Corrie could hardly wait through morning roll call to hear the list of prisoners to be released. But there was no list that day. She stumbled off to the Phillips factory, as depressed as she had been at any time since she had arrived in the camp. How she had waited for this day. She forced herself to be more alert. She prayed to Jesus for courage. Where else would she get it? She had to have it. This was a dangerous time. Prisoners who gave up hope seemed to have terrible accidents.

That night Betsie consoled her, "The notice of our release may be a day or two late. The Nazis seem to be distracted now."

Sweet Betsie. Who was more vulnerable than she? And yet she had to console Corrie. Corrie was ashamed. But she did have a feeling of dread. They had to get their freedom now. If they didn't, two terrible choices awaited them: execution here or winter in Germany.

After another two days Betsie said, "Maybe they started our sentence when we arrived here at the camp. What would that make our release date?"

Corrie figured furiously. "December 9!" she said, not so triumphantly. Where would they be then? Every night now she prayed for God's help more desperately. The madness of the Nazis was overwhelming her. Oh, the injustice. What if they were taken to Germany at the last moment before their release? What if they were executed? The terrible injustice. Only Christ's suffering—so much worse than her own—kept her from giving up.

Rumors rampaged through the camps now: the British and Americans had captured Brussels. Belgium was almost free again. Holland would soon be free! No. Brussels was still in the clutches of the Nazis. No, the British and Americans had Brussels but they were going to bypass Holland and thrust straight to the black heart of Germany. No, the British and Americans were going to free Holland first.

The prisoners took each rumor and extrapolated. The latrine was crowded with orators. If Holland was bypassed, their life would not change that much. No, in that case the guards would take it out on the prisoners. If Holland was attacked, they would be executed: the Nazis had no time for prisoners. No, they would be evacuated to Germany: Hitler was a madman bent on revenge. No, they would be freed: the Nazis wanted leniency after they lost the war. On and on went the arguments. . . .

One morning there was no roll call.

A guard burst into the barracks long after they were usually up. "Get your things together!" she screamed in a frightened voice.

The women heard the dreaded *pop-pop-pop* from the men's camp. Were the men being executed? What was happening? Were the Americans and British attacking? Perhaps they parachuted during the night! The women were marched into a field. There, unbelievably, passing out blankets, a German soldier stood in the bed of an Army truck. A thousand women filed past and each took a blanket. But hadn't they just left blankets in the camp?

They marched out of the camp five abreast. As they passed through the gates Corrie saw the same rough wooded path they had walked three months ago. They marched to the same railroad tracks. Soldiers lined them up along the track three deep. They waited, clutching their blankets and pillowcases stuffed with belongings. They whispered excitedly. Were they going back the same way? Would they ride that same train back to The Hague? Praise the Lord.

Betsie grabbed Corrie's arm. "Look. There is no passenger train here. Only a freight train."

Far down the track were men prisoners. Maybe there were no executions. Who could know for sure? Some women were saying 180 had been shot. Some were saying 700. Some were saying none. Who could know the truth in the Nazi madness? On top of the freight cars were German soldiers with machine guns. Other soldiers were walking alongside the train, stopping at each car, throwing the bolt lock, then sliding the door open.

After they opened the door to the car nearest Corrie, a red-faced soldier yelled, *"Schnell! Gehen sie weg!"*

Women were forced inside the freight cars! Helping them climb up through the door, the soldiers were soon breathless from laughing and grabbing handfuls of unwilling flesh as the women scrambled awkwardly into the freight car. Corrie flailed at their steely groping fingers. She swatted their filthy hands off Betsie. The prettier the woman the more outrageously they pinched and groped her.

A soldier growled at one woman in German, "Goodbye, troublemaker. You will soon know what trouble is!"

The car stunk of mildewed grain. The women were all standing up on the rough wooden floor of the car. But the soldiers kept adding women until they stood so close together Corrie had to wonder how they would ever rest. Suddenly they were plunged into blackness. The bolt slammed shut on the door. They were locked in!

"Oh Jesus, save us," prayed Corrie.

"Thank God Papa is in heaven," said Betsie.

Somehow in the darkness they found rest. They sat like members of a bobsled team, their legs wrapped around the hips of the woman in front of them. Buffered by blankets it was almost tolerable, except for the heat. Those on the sides attacked the walls. They had to have air. With anything they could find they gouged tiny holes until sunlight appeared.

The train lurched ahead—its destination unknown to the inmates. When Corrie got her turn at an air hole she saw the night sky. She was on the right side of the train. There was Antares in the southern sky. She remembered her astronomy from the Triangle Club. They were traveling east—into Germany. She couldn't bring herself to tell Betsie. They were already in hell.

The air in the car grew more foul. If there were buckets for waste in her part of the car she knew nothing about them. Somewhere in the car bread was stored because it was being passed around. But the smell in the car was nauseating. It would be a long time before Corrie could eat her piece of bread in that stench. And she was very thirsty.

Each day the car seemed hotter and hotter.

Suddenly one day they were blinded. A guard opened the door and ordered them out. They were too stiff to stand up and walk. They crawled to the light and fell out the opening like blind crabs, clutching blankets and pillowcases. They sprawled like fish on a bank gasping for air, praying for water. Yes, someone had a pail. There was a lake nearby, someone said. The stronger ones began to crawl toward the lake. Corrie stayed with Betsie. Finally her eyes adjusted to the sunshine. She made sure Betsie got water when pails of water finally worked their way back to the weak ones still sprawled by the tracks.

Their guards were young boys in baggy uniforms, standing far off, repelled by the stinking women.

"Where are we?" yelled a woman in German.

"Furstenburg," replied a scowling boy.

"Furstenburg? Where is Furstenburg?" asked another woman.

"Southeast of Berlin, you stupid cow," snapped a boy.

"Thanks, you miserable brat," muttered the woman in Dutch.

Corrie looked at Betsie. Yes, she was pitying the boys. That was Betsie. She was merely seeing more Nazi victims. If Betsie had been strong enough she probably would have been on her feet organizing a prayer meeting among the boys. But she looked very old today, far older than her fifty-nine years. More white showed under her pupils than ever before. Her sunken chest was heaving. She had scarcely moved since Corrie tried to soften her fall from the freight car.

"Get up, you cows!" screamed the boy who was still angry because the women had not known of tiny Furstenburg's fame.

The boys marched them along the shore of the lake, then up a hill. The men prisoners were nowhere to be seen. The plodding women passed a few farmers and their families on the way. The country folk were red-cheeked, dressed in feathered caps and lederhosen. Could such people live their wonderfully pure lives these days? It seemed impossible. And it was Betsie who reminded Corrie their good fortune was probably an illusion.

"That family has probably lost a brother, an uncle, a son somewhere in the mud of Russia," she said sympathetically.

When the women reached the crest of the hill they saw their new camp down in the next valley. It was not a scar in the woods like Vught. This camp was a cancer, the trees having been cleared far back from the enclosure which was not a wire fence but a concrete wall with strands of wire at the top. Inside the wall stretched dozens and dozens of cold gray barracks. A tall stack fouled the blue sky with smoke.

As they got closer, Corrie could see the strands strung along the top of the concrete wall were not barbed wire. "Electrified Wire" warned the signs in German. Guard towers were spaced along the wall.

Corrie called to Floor, "What is this place?"

"Hell on earth." The blood seemed to have drained completely from Floor's face. "I think this must be Ravensbruck."

Ravensbruck!

Any woman imprisoned in Holland by the Nazis had heard of Ravensbruck. Especially those women who had worked in the underground. Ravensbruck was not just a camp for women, but a camp for women who were considered incorrigible by the Nazis. It was a work camp. But the rumor was that the inmates were worked to death. There was no way out. Ever.

Betsie smiled bravely. "It's not hopeless, Corrie. The Russians might bust through. They might overwhelm the camp at any moment. They couldn't be too far away, you know."

Did Betsie's optimism ever waver? Betsie looked haggard. Her glasses were broken again. Nollie's blue sweater under her overalls draped on her like a bag. Her wrists looked as thin as sticks and as white as ivory.

Once inside the massive gates the guards drove the one

day after day, often pointlessly standing at attention until their knees trembled. Those who collapsed were taken away and not seen again. No one complained. They were veterans of Nazi inhumanity. It took the Nazis days and days to process prisoners. Besides, waiting must be better than working in this place. And anything was better than the hell of the freight cars.

"Oh please, Jesus," prayed Corrie, "don't let us suffer anything worse than the freight cars."

Lice at Ravensbruck were not a new problem. It was their abundance that was alarming. The ground swarmed with lice. The women had no choice. Their hair had to go. The guards did not insist on it. The women did it themselves.

"Oh, Betsie, your beautiful chestnut hair," cried Corrie as she sheared the wavy locks off her sister.

Betsie looked so inconsequential with her tired shorn head wobbling on a thin goose neck. Never had she looked so frail, so wispy, so marginally alive. Betsie was silent as her hands snipped Corrie's hair. As the locks fell to the ground Corrie was shocked. Her thick dark blond hair was now streaked white!

They surrendered their names too. Betsie was now Number 66729. Corrie was Number 66730. More of the reality of Ravensbruck soon hit them. They were asked to surrender all their belongings.

"But your own soldiers in Holland just gave us these blankets," protested one woman.

"Shut up!" A guard slapped the woman. "Apparently the soldiers who have been vacationing on the western front enjoy more luxuries than we do."

So the prisoners speculated the German soldiers fighting Russia were truly desperate. Why would they take second-hand blankets of prisoners otherwise? But Corrie was not gloating. She was fearful of losing their possessions. Betsie needed Nollie's sweater. And the vitamins. And how could they live without their Bible?

The one thousand women lined up. The guards were shuttling fifty at a time into the shower room. Before they went into the shower room they surrendered their possessions. Farther on in the line the women stripped and dumped their clothing into a second pile. They then walked naked past several deadly-serious guards into the shower. These guards were not leering. They were tired of this place, of these emaciated lice-infested women. They hated it. When the women reappeared from the shower room each one wore a threadbare prison dress and leather shoes.

Before her group reached the first pile of abandoned possessions Corrie clutched the bottle of vitamins in her hand. Then she and Betsie dropped their blankets and pillow cases into the pile. How it hurt to surrender their nice blankets, combs, needles, thread, all the things they had so painstakingly collected over six months. But they still had their most precious possessions: vitamins, Betsie's sweater, and the Bible.

"Oh please, Jesus," prayed Corrie, "please allow us to keep Your precious Word."

CHAPTER 11

Suddenly Betsie doubled over, seized by a severe cramp.

"Please, sir," Corrie implored the guard in German, "she has diarrhea."

The guard scowled in disgust. "Well, don't let her do it here! Get her out of my sight. Go in there." He jabbed his finger at the shower room.

Corrie rushed Betsie into the shower room. It was empty! They were between groups. Corrie quickly took the sweater from Betsie, wrapped the Bible and bottle of vitamins in the sweater and hid the bundle behind a wooden bench crawling with roaches. Stacked in the other end of the shower room were the dresses and shoes they were to wear.

They returned to the line, shed their clothes, and Corrie imagined to herself no one saw them as they walked past the guards. Inside the shower room, after the short icy blast, they dressed in their new camp garb—plus one sweater, one bottle of vitamins and one Bible. But their problems were not over. The Bible in the pouch hanging from Corrie's neck on a string was not well concealed under the flimsy dress.

She had no choice but to pray again. "Oh please, Jesus, protect me. Surround me with your angels."

They marched slowly past guards who made no effort to hide their disgust as they searched every woman from head to toe with groping hands. Rough hands covered the woman in front of Corrie. Rough hands covered Betsie behind Corrie. No hands touched Corrie. It was as if she were invisible.

Corrie was so grateful to God she barely heard a woman say, "I spent a couple of years in Germany when I was a girl."

"So what?" asked her neighbor suspiciously.

"I'll tell you why. Every night in January there is a hard freeze."

"It freezes in Holland too."

"Not like here. Many nights here the temperature drops below zero."

Below zero! Was winter going to be that frigid?

Finally the guards marched them into the main camp and prodded them ten abreast past the permanent barracks. The small army would stop while several numbers were called, thinning their ranks, then continue. Corrie and Betsie stopped at Barracks 28. A not-very-happy guard briskly led them and several other newcomers, including Mien, straight into the dormitory.

"What a smell!" blurted Betsie.

"Ignore it, you cow," growled the guard. "There are worse things in here than that."

Perhaps one could learn to ignore the stink of rotting straw. Could one ignore the sour stench of vomit and human waste? And this dormitory seemed a hellish congestion of square platforms stacked three deep and covered by straw. The platforms were crammed together so that one aisle had to serve many platforms. Corrie and Betsie would have to crawl across three platforms to reach their own platform. What Corrie and Betsie did not know yet was how many women shared each platform square.

The guard quickly took the newcomers to a central

ting Army socks from gray wool. "Get to work," said the
guard, who no longer seemed to be in a hurry. Half a dozen
other guards moved listlessly around the room.

Corrie and Betsie sat down. Corrie whispered in German to a woman next to her, "Is this a knitting barracks?"

"No. The others are out working."

"How many live here?"

"Fourteen hundred. The barracks are supposed to hold
four hundred."

"How many are in the camp?" asked Corrie.

"They say 35,000," the woman answered lifelessly.

The other prisoners returned at six o'clock. The last
thing they wanted to talk about was work. But Corrie and
Betsie did learn a few things as they drank a tasteless broth
with shreds of cabbage floating in it. They learned prisoners were from all over Europe. At first the camp had been
full of Poles, Finns and Russians. Now women flooded in
from everywhere as the Nazis were being pushed back on
all fronts. The barracks held Dutch, French, Belgians, Danes,
Norwegians and even some poor mysterious women no
one in the barracks could communicate with at all.

"How terribly sad," said Betsie.

That night they learned more stark truths. Their half of
the dormitory had eight toilets for seven hundred women.
They shared the platform with seven other women, who
were not happy about their arrival. A crash nearby and
screams and curses informed them the slats under the straw
were very unstable. And a sting told Corrie they shared the
platform with more than other women.

"Fleas!" cried Corrie as she slapped at the source of
the sting.

"Remember First Thessalonians?" asked Betsie.

"Why?"

"It says, 'Give thanks in all circumstances.' "

"Am I supposed to give thanks for fleas?" she asked sarcastically.

"Yes."

"Shut up!" screamed someone. "You must be in the knitting brigade not to want to go to sleep."

Somehow Corrie fell asleep in spite of the flea bites. She was awakened by a whistle. Choking dust filled the air as women scrambled off the platforms for black bread and coffee in the knitting room. Slowpokes found little left.

"What time is it?" asked Corrie, chewing the tough bread. "Didn't we just fall asleep?"

"Four o'clock. Same time it was at this time yesterday," grumbled someone.

At four-thirty, fourteen hundred women stood outside Barracks 28 under street lights for roll call. To Corrie it represented a further decline of their fortunes. At Vught they had roll call at five o'clock. Amazingly, Corrie and Betsie marched with several thousand other women right out of the massive gates of the camp, across the barren area and into the woods!

"We're going to the Siemens factory," grunted a woman to Corrie's obvious question.

"What do they make?"

"Not cotton balls," said one woman bitterly.

The work at the Siemens factory was backbreaking. It was one of the great iron and steel works of Germany. Corrie and Betsie had to push a handcart to a door at the factory where German civilians loaded it with heavy metal plates. The civilians refused to look at the prisoners. Then Corrie and Betsie threw their weak middle-aged bodies against the loaded cart to push it along a dock where they finally stopped it by a boxcar. They tried to get their breath as they helped load the plates into the boxcar.

At lunch each prisoner feasted on one boiled potato and a cup of broth. "Praise the Lord," said Betsie weakly. "I heard in the camp they get nothing for lunch."

Betsie could hardly walk the mile and a half back to camp, and guards were quick to lash out at stragglers. They wanted their day to end as quickly as possible. After a dinner of turnip soup Betsie recovered enough for the most important moments of the day. They found a light bulb in the dormitory and read from the Bible. The first night those who had come with them from Vught joined them, along with a few of the curious.

Corrie was worried. Wouldn't it attract a guard? But strangely, guards were almost never seen in the dormitory of Barracks 28. Corrie asked an inmate, "Why do the guards never come in the dormitory?"

"They are repelled by the fleas."

That night Corrie thanked God for the fleas as she fell asleep. Each day seemed the same. Betsie got weaker and weaker as they toiled at the Siemens factory. Then she got stronger and stronger as they read the Bible in the evenings. The nightly readings attracted more and more listeners too. It was no longer enough to read the Bible in Dutch. Corrie would translate the passage into German. Another woman would repeat it in Russian. Another in Danish. Another in French. And on and on went God's true Word in the world's stumbling tongues.

Another marvelous thing that happened to them was the miracle of the vitamin bottle. It never seemed to run out of drops of liquid. Corrie was just certain it had to be exhausted. But it wasn't. She fretted about it all the time. Betsie depended on the vitamins to fight her anemia. And to worry Corrie even more, Betsie shared the bottle with everyone who asked.

Betsie just shrugged. "Don't you remember in First Kings the story of Elijah and the widow of Zaraphath of Sidon?"

Corrie blinked. "The widow who had the jar of flour and the jug of oil? And they both seemed almost empty, yet never ran out. . . ." But Corrie worried anyway. If only she had Betsie's faith.

"Tonight you can relax," said Mien one evening.

She pressed something into Corrie's hand. It was a new bottle of vitamins! Once again wonderful little Mien had somehow attached herself to a nurse and was scrounging things for the inmates. And that very night the old bottle of vitamins ran out of drops. It was bone dry.

"Do God's miracles never cease? Oh God, I do believe," said Corrie.

In November they were issued coats. No more work details went to the Siemens factory. Why the work there stopped was a mystery. But bombs were dropping in the vicinity every night and the great iron and steel works was probably a prime target. And Ravensbruck was not that far from the most prime target of all: Berlin—the heart of the German Reich—if such a monstrosity had a heart.

In the camp Corrie and Betsie were put to work leveling rough ground close to the concrete wall. Shoveling dirt was grueling on the best of days. But this day was after a hard rain and shoveling the water-soaked soil felt like shoveling lead. Betsie's health was failing. She could hardly lift her shovel. Corrie eyed the guard. Would the guard notice how little Betsie was doing?

Suddenly the guard was glaring at Betsie!

CHAPTER 12

"**W**hy are you not working harder?" screamed the guard at Betsie. "That's nothing but a spoonful of dirt on your shovel."

"I'm sorry," Betsie answered good-naturedly, "but even spoonfuls add up."

If the other prisoners hadn't laughed Betsie probably would have been all right. But no one swollen with pride can stand laughter. The guard struck Betsie with a leather crop. Betsie was bleeding. Her precious blood, of which she had so little, was streaming into the void. Corrie wanted to kill the guard. Betsie grabbed her arm before she could swing her shovel.

That night Betsie said, "I saw the hatred in your face." She quickly changed the subject, "Perhaps we will be released December 9. Remember? That's six months after we entered Vught."

"Of course," agreed Corrie, hiding her disbelief.

Rain and cold worsened Betsie's health. She now coughed blood. Again and again Corrie supported Betsie while she escorted her to the infirmary. Again and again the effort was in vain. Only a fever of 104 degrees got medical attention. Sick call itself was dangerous. The women stood in line outside in the elements for hours before they were examined.

One day Betsie reached the threshold. She was finally admitted to the infirmary. Betsie returned to Barracks 28 three days later. No doctor had ever seen her. No medicine had ever been given to her. She still had a fever. But the visit was not in vain. She was rested. And somehow she had been transferred to the knitting room. The general health of the women was so poor now that the knitting brigade overflowed into the dormitories. The dormitory was paradise for Betsie. Even ill, she could knit so fast she finished her quota of socks by noon. And because a guard rarely ventured into the dormitory she could move among the knitting brigade with the Gospel.

"What bliss," she told Corrie.

One day Corrie joined Betsie. She had learned in three months at Ravensbruck that the guards could not keep track of 35,000 women. Corrie simply walked away from roll call to stroll into the central room like she belonged there, grabbed a skein of gray wool and joined the knitting brigade in the dormitory. Betsie began to speak with glowing eyes of a mission after the war. They would help people who were warped by the war find Jesus. There would be millions of them. She and Corrie would live with them. But not at the Beje. It wasn't big enough for Betsie's mission. She had envisioned a mansion in Haarlem. She could even describe the inlaid wood of its golden floors and the manicured gardens that surrounded it. There was a gallery around a central hall. Bas-relief statutes adorned the walls. There were tall leaded windows, a gabled roof. Corrie was stunned by the vivid vision. It seemed Betsie was standing right there in Haarlem looking at it.

"You seem on a higher plain now—with Christ," she told Betsie.

Corrie was trying to get there too. Yet she knew she was so flawed. But wasn't that conviction of sin a first step to redemption and living in Christ? She hoped and prayed that it was because every day revealed a flaw. One night she did not want to share a blanket with a newcomer. One morning she maneuvered herself into the middle of their formation for roll call, so she wouldn't get so cold near the edge. She hoarded the bottle of vitamins. Her Bible reading was mechanical. She read the words with her head, but not her heart. What was happening to her? The closer Betsie got to God the more Corrie drifted away!

At least she knew she was straying. "Oh Jesus, help me. I'm sinking."

One December day a passage from Paul's second letter to the Corinthians fairly exploded in her mind: For Christ's sake, I delight in weaknesses, in insults, in hardships, in persecutions, in difficulties. For when I am weak, then I am strong. Her mistake was in thinking she had power. Jesus was the one in power. And the weaker she became the stronger Christ became. She could see it so plainly in Betsie's case. And now in her own case too.

As blessed as Betsie's life was in the dormitory she could not escape the dreaded roll calls twice a day. In December the air iced their bones and all too often they were kept at roll call until prisoners started keeling over. December 9 came and passed. They still hoped to be released. One week before Christmas Betsie could not move off the platform for morning roll call. Once again she disappeared into the infirmary. Maybe this time Betsie would get the medicine she needed. One dreary day at noon—Corrie didn't even know if Christmas had come yet or not—she slipped away from her work detail. She crept around the infirmary until she found the window looking in on Betsie's ward. Dear Betsie was lying on a cot. Corrie tapped on the pane.

Betsie opened her eyes, very tired, probably sedated.

She tried to smile. She nodded "yes" after Corrie mouthed, "Are you all right?"

Praise the Lord, Betsie was resting, out of the cold. She was only fifty-nine, but she had never been strong. She had a miraculously productive life for someone who was virtually a invalid. But why was Corrie thinking such final thoughts? Betsie would recover. They would be freed. They would open their mission. She just knew it. After all, Betsie had a vision. And God didn't make mistakes.

The next day she sneaked back. Where was Betsie? On the cot was the corpse of an old woman, completely naked. She was pitifully thin. Yellow skin stretched over bone. The hair was matted. It was so sad. But where was Betsie? Was Betsie up and about all already? It seemed too much to ask. What was that by the cot? Nollie's blue sweater?

The truth hammered her. "The dead woman is Betsie!"

She stumbled from the window and wandered in a daze. Betsie! Dead! How was it possible? Her dear sweet older sister whom she had seen almost every day of her life for fifty-two years. And now she was dead. She had just weakened second by second, day after day, week after week, month after month, and slipped away to Jesus. If only they had been released September 1! Or even December 9. Sweet Betsie would have lived. But what had Betsie told her when the terrible occupation began? There are no "ifs" in God's world. But what of Betsie's vision? How could Corrie make sense of it now? Betsie was gone.

"Corrie! Come quick," urged a voice.

It was Mien. Mien held her arm, gently urging her back to the infirmary.

Corrie couldn't go back there again. "Don't you know what happened?" she asked numbly.

"You must see this." And Mien guided her to a window.

The sight inside stunned her.

Betsie was lying there, transformed. Her skin was no longer yellow but ivory. She no longer had drab matted hair but neat chestnut locks. She was no longer skeletal but wonderfully formed. Her face was serene, at perfect peace. And why not? She was with the Lord in heaven.

"Oh, thank You, Jesus," cried Corrie. And she let herself grieve. She was missing sweet Betsie, of course. But Betsie was not lost, but found.

It was Betsie's vision that troubled Corrie. Betsie was gone. To paradise, yes. But why had she told Corrie her vision so many times? Because Corrie no longer believed she was going to survive either. How many roll calls in icy wind could her disintegrating body withstand? She had long ago lost the weight she gained at Vught. How much punishment could one undernourished bag of bones take?

January would be even worse than December. She remembered the woman's warning: zero degrees! Her blood was frozen slush now. The strong ones stomped their feet during roll call to keep from freezing. But eventually one became too weak—like sweet Betsie—to do that. Corrie saw how swollen her own legs and feet had become. Her shoes were ridiculous flaps of leather. It only took one small cold which became a bad cold with drainage which became raging pneumonia which became a woman's last rattling breath.

"Jesus, help me," she prayed. "I must not give up hope." She must never think Betsie suffered a long time in vain. Sweet Betsie had changed the lives of so many inmates. But what if none of the prisoners survived? What was the point? The point was, she reminded herself, to save them in Jesus and get them to heaven. Corrie must not lose sight of Betsie's great victory—which was really the victory of Jesus.

One morning at roll call the guard called out, "Corrie ten Boom. Fall out!"

Not "Number 66730!" But "Corrie ten Boom." What did it mean? She was no fool. Some of the older women did not die. They simply disappeared. It was a horror no one talked about. Inmates talked about almost everything—but not that smokestack. There was never the sound of gun shots. One wouldn't need a bullet to kill an inmate of Ravensbruck. They were so weak a sharp blow to the head would do it. Besides they only had to be unconscious before they were fed into the furnace!

Ironically, after all the waiting and hoping, it was no comfort to Corrie to have her name called at morning roll call. The Nazis were such devils. She smelled a trap when she was taken for a medical examination. A doctor made her stay in the infirmary and be treated for edema. She couldn't deny her feet and ankles were horribly swollen. But she had never been more suspicious. The Nazis were slow, bungling, ugly—but as certain as cancer. This ward may be no more than a holding area until the Nazis could work through their backlog of undesirables at the furnace.

Still, she must not give up hope.

Yet doubt gnawed at her. If she were released just as the Russians arrived would she ever get back to Holland anyway? She would be behind the Russian army. But she must not think that way. There are no "ifs" in God's world.

Her heart was in her mouth the morning they marched her away from the infirmary to a shed near the outskirts of the camp. Was it 1944 or 1945? She wasn't sure.

A guard sneered. "Step inside the dressing shed."

Was this to be her last moment on earth?

CHAPTER 13

"Is this possible?" she muttered a few minutes later.

She stood, dressed in civilian clothes, waiting for the massive gates to swing open. She even had her Alpina watch, gold ring and Dutch guilders. The world of the Nazis was truly insane. With others she marched numbly back up the hill toward the railroad tracks where she and Betsie had arrived four months earlier. When she reached the crest she didn't look back. The group of inmates followed the iron rails into the village of Furstenburg. Where were the screaming guards? The agony of leather strops? She waited numbly in the small train station, then climbed into a boxcar with other Dutch women. After that it was a succession of confusing rail yards and switching boxcars. It would be a miracle if they made it back to Holland.

Many days later they heard a man shout, "Nieuweschans!"

Nieuweschans was in Holland! Could it be true? Soon after that the train rolled into Groningen and stopped. It was the end of the line. The rest of Holland's rail system was destroyed. Corrie limped with others to a Christian hospital called the Deaconess Home. After ten days of recuperation there in luxury she had forgotten existed she got a midnight ride on a food truck. Farmers were trucking their produce illegally all over Holland in darkness. Many Dutch in the cities were starving.

In Hilversum she saw Willem again. Even he, who considered death a mere step into glory, slumped when he heard Betsie was gone. Corrie soon learned how much Willem's own family had suffered. His son Kik had been caught and hauled away by the Nazis. Willem himself was yellow-skinned. He had contracted some kind of crippling disease of the spine in the prison at Scheveningen. But he was just like Betsie. He acted as if he were going to live another thirty years.

One February day of 1945 Corrie was back at the Beje, even though the Nazis still occupied Haarlem. A woman stepped out the door.

"Nollie!" screamed Corrie.

"Corrie!"

Through a flood of tears the sisters hugged each other while Nollie's daughters gathered around, chattering like happy larks. The Beje was fine—as long as Nollie and her happy girls were there with her. But after they left, it was so lonely. The stolen typewriter, rugs, watches and clocks nagged at Corrie. But what were they compared to poor Betsie? And poor Papa? Grief overwhelmed her.

"I must get busy again," she said.

She tried to occupy herself with the watch shop. But Betsie's vision swelled up inside her. Now was the time. Corrie was free, back in Haarlem. What was her excuse? Betsie's vision could not be neglected. But where would Corrie find the mansion of Betsie's vision? And who would she talk to about the war? And who would want to listen? The Nazis were still here. But she began speaking anyway—to clubs, to people in their homes, to anyone who would listen anywhere at any time. It took only a few talks and she felt God had told her exactly what to say. She had to point out that no pit was too deep for someone who was safe in Jesus. She described every degrading detail of imprisonment, so people would know how deep the pit was. She described Betsie's vision. The Dutch must care for all the poor victims who were scarred by prisons and camps. The Dutch must give them a chance to find Jesus.

Often a woman would approach her after her talk and whisper, "Can't you wait? There are still Nazis here. . . ."

So when a woman, dressed in such elegance that she appeared untouched by the war, approached her after one talk, Corrie expected the usual warning. But the woman said, "I'm Mrs. Bierens de Haan. I live in a very large house in Bloemendaal. But now I am a widow. All my children are grown. I would like to give up my house for your sister's vision."

Corrie was leery. "Are you sure?"

"It was a revelation to me, right out of the blue."

Corrie sighed. "My sister had a very specific place in mind." Corrie hoped she didn't sound like an ingrate. But she wouldn't be lying about what Betsie said. "This house of Betsie's has a golden floor of inlaid wood. Beautiful manicured gardens surround it. There must be a gallery around a central hall. The walls must be adorned by bas-relief statutes. There is a wonderful gabled roof with tall leaded windows—" She stopped. The woman's mouth was gaping. Corrie prayed the woman wouldn't say too many bad things later about her haughty demands.

The woman gasped, "That's my house you've described!"

So they opened a home for those unfortunate minds mangled by prisons and concentration camps. Holland's liberation seemed almost anticlimactic. Suddenly the Nazis were gone. The streets were full of soldiers from Canada. She knew in her head it was a great day for

Holland. But in her heart she knew really great days were when people found the Light. Corrie seemed to be operating on a new level. To make sure she was deserving she studied the Bible as she never had before. She didn't want to make any mistakes.

One of the first insights she had was that she had to forgive. Everyone. Even the dreadful Nazis. Even the Dutch traitors. Even the despised Dutchman from Ermelo! But after she did, her mind seemed free of hate and revenge. Once again, God was right. God was always right. Why did people resist him so? She thought long and hard about how she must determine God's will for herself. God did not speak to her directly. She was no saint. He did not make it easy for her. Life is not a cartoon. Doors opened and doors closed and those who have eyes must look hard, those who have ears must listen hard.

Even Nollie was not prepared for Corrie's next move. "You're going where?" she asked Corrie in disbelief.

"I'm going to America," said Corrie.

"But what about the Beje?" asked Nollie.

"Betsie would be sad if she knew I was using up my precious time for anything but delivering her message about the victory of Jesus in the concentration camps. I'm turning the Beje into a home for victims of the war. The rehabilitation center in Bloemendaal is overflowing."

"But they say it is impossible to get to America. The waiting list for a passenger ship is a year at least. And you need a lot of money to live in America, Corrie."

"I have fifty dollars. If God does not want me to go, the gate will be closed for me. But if He does want me to go, the gate will open. . . ."

Corrie did go to America. In New York City she got a room at the YWCA. Every morning she went out, bought her one meal of the day—coffee, orange juice and a donut —then trudged all day long through the long canyons of Manhattan, knocking on every church door. Some treated her like a beggar. Some told her no one wanted to talk about the war any more. But what were those obstacles to a survivor of the Nazi concentration camps? Even a wrenching letter from Nollie didn't stop her. Willem had died. And they learned Kik had died in a work camp in Germany. But by sheer persistence Corrie met a few movers and shakers in the American churches before she returned to Holland.

"I'll come back to America too," she promised herself.

Her next foray was even more startling: Germany! She and Betsie had talked about how they would like to go back to Germany some day and paint the prison barracks bright colors and plant flowers. They had to help the poor sick guards, the tiny nasty cogs in the insane Nazi machine, to find new lives through Jesus. Their rehabilitation was important too. Any dream of Betsie's was reality to Corrie. And at Darmstadt, southeast of Frankfurt, Corrie helped a church organization renovate a concentration camp.

The world forgave the Germans, as Corrie had. Help and money poured in. After a while, Corrie saw the rehabilitation of Germany well under way. There were other places to go to deliver her message about Jesus. Her evangelizing seemed wildly impulsive. She would establish herself and her message in one country, then abruptly leave to go somewhere else. She refused money. Money was not always offered for the right reasons. Corrie became like the Apostle Paul. She arrived, she worked, she preached the Gospel, and she accepted whatever anyone wanted to give her. A bed. A meal. But not money.

She proudly introduced herself, "I am a 'tramp for the Lord.'"

For years she traveled alone, brazenly intruding on lives, preaching the Gospel: in South Africa, Japan, Bermuda, New Zealand, Australia, Spain, England, Denmark, Formosa, Israel. Ten countries, twenty countries, thirty, forty, fifty, sixty! She did return to America and Germany. She wrote books too. Her anecdotes sold well. The royalties from the books were pumped into her work. She bought another house in Haarlem, which became another center for rehabilitation. She went there to rest occasionally. She was no celebrity anywhere, but especially in Holland. Too many others had endured the same experience to be awed by her courage. Nollie's death in 1953 at sixty-three stunned her. Now Corrie's generation of the family was dead except for herself. Corrie had idolized her sisters and Willem.

"Why do I, the least deserving, remain?" she asked God.

Year after year she traveled. As she got older and more feeble, younger women accompanied her. They went to Africa, India, Argentina, Korea, eastern Europe, Russia—countries in every continent. Her travels took her to some places too dangerous to believe. . . .

CHAPTER 14

Ping! Ping!

"Old lady, don't you know those are bullets whizzing by us?" asked American soldiers in Vietnam, startled to see Corrie crawling creakily out of a jeep to deliver the Gospel.

"I've heard them before," she said as bullets whizzed and snicked through the foliage.

Who could believe this old lady was now in the midst of civil wars in Africa too? Traveling was hard for a woman in her seventies. More and more often she was tempted to quit. Didn't she deserve to rest at her age? Giving speech after speech tired her. And after most speeches she and her companion sat a table selling her books and tapes.

In the late 1960s a writing team told Corrie how excited they were by her book about Ravensbruck called *A Prisoner and Yet*. "But we were sure there is even a bigger story to be told!"

Soon Corrie was collaborating with them on a book emphasizing her war experiences from 1939 to 1944. The book was to be called *The Hiding Place*. The title referred to two hiding places: the secret room or "angels' crib" where the ten Boom family hid refugees from the Nazis, and Jesus, in whom Corrie hid when events were crushing her. Published in 1971, the book was no narration of dry facts, but a first-person cliff-hanger.

It sold very well. And Corrie gave away thousands of copies to strangers as she asked, "Do you know Jesus?"

In 1974 Corrie collaborated with another writer on a sequel to *The Hiding Place* called *Tramp for the Lord.* American friends incorporated her as "Christians, Inc." to free her of red tape and the necessity to manage her money. Corrie still traveled the globe. Money meant little more to her than buying air fare for herself and her companion to their next destination. In 1975 Billy Graham's World Wide Pictures filmed *The Hiding Place* on locations in England and Holland. That same year, at eighty-three, she finished collaborating on a third major book, *In My Father's House,* which she explained was about her "early years finding Jesus."

Billy Graham tried to convince her that personal appearances were no longer the most effective way for her to spread the Gospel. They were necessary at the beginning of her calling, but now they actually limited her impact. Her influence would be greater through films and television and books. But she still wanted to travel the globe and talk to groups too. Spreading the message "Jesus is Victor" was so personal. But things had changed for Corrie. Now she had fans. Many were celebrity worshippers. They exploded flash bulbs in her face in the middle of her presentation.

"Please don't do that," she would protest. "This is about Jesus. Not me."

And her companion now had to fend off fans who tried to grab Corrie around the neck to hug her. She finally admitted to herself itinerant preaching was too difficult with these new exuberant fans. And she had a troubling dream now too. She was locked in a room with no way out. It seemed a warning that her time was short. She must channel her flagging energies into short films and writing books.

In 1977 she moved into a ranch style home in the Los Angeles area in California. She celebrated her eighty-fifth birthday there. In her remaining years she planned to do five books and five movie shorts. Of course Corrie made other commitments. It was only natural after she finished her short prison film, *One Way Door*, that she start a neighborhood group praying weekly for prisoners. Naturally she had to be at the prayer meeting herself. And when she got an invitation to the prison at San Quentin how could she refuse to go? And when people showed up at her house saying God sent them there how could Corrie refuse to see them? Still, by December Corrie had finished the first of her five books, *Each New Day*, and stopped long enough to get a pacemaker. She celebrated her eighty-sixth birthday while making a film with Christian Indians in Arizona. In the summer of 1978 she made a third film, *Jesus is Victor*, and was honored in Denver on an episode of "This is Your Life" for television. Each venture now required more recuperation. Often Corrie saw fatigue or botched plans as an attack by the devil.

"Let us pray," she cried. "We are not fighting against flesh and blood but against principalities and powers. There is a devil, much stronger than I, but there is Jesus, much stronger than the devil, and with the help of Jesus I will win!"

Following an unrelenting schedule Corrie reached her goal of five books and five movie shorts in less than two years. Then one morning in August of 1978 when she woke up she couldn't move. All her memories of Mama's paralysis flooded back. Now here was Corrie sixty years later. Her troubling dream of being locked in a room had come true. . . .

CHAPTER 15

For five years Corrie fought paralysis. Sometimes she improved, then she faltered again. Her life was mostly a pleasant indulgence. She watched birds at the bird feeder in the garden behind the house. She did needlework. She listened to Bach. Her favorite Bible, the English translation by J. B. Phillips, was read to her several times a day. She prayed with her companion. She received a few visitors. She went on drives in a car. She was able to put together another devotional book by indicating her choices from many clippings she had saved over the years. But the old peppery evangelizing days were over. And sometimes she wept in frustration. She was almost ninety-years old.

"Why keep me here so long, God? Why?"

But she would remember Mama's paralysis and her unbounded love. Love triumphs over all afflictions. Earthly sufferings only serve to make that which awaits us an even greater glory. And so she poured out her love to everyone around her.

Soon she was completely bedridden, her speech almost nonexistent, her arms and hands limp rags. During a Bible reading she might raise her arms to heaven if a truth struck her forcefully. But mostly she lay immobile as she listened to music or Bible readings or prayers. In evenings they gave her slide shows of the sixty-six countries and hundreds of dear friends she had visited. She had 7000 slides! She seemed to have lived a dozen lives. Occasionally the futility of her existence overwhelmed her and she wept. *Why keep me here so long, God? Why?* Again, she would remember Mama and her suffering and the indescribable glory that awaited the faithful. The next moment she was radiating love again to the others.

One day she had a marvelous vision of the Lord. It seemed as rich as Revelation. It had to be the third paradise the Apostle Paul could not write about. She managed to convey this experience to her companions. Corrie lived on and on. She experienced visions. She experienced despair. Eventually, she could not open her eyes. She had little left but her hearing. The last thing she heard was someone reading the 103rd Psalm, a Dutch tradition for birthdays. "But from everlasting to everlasting the Lord's love is with those who fear him."

And Corrie passed into glory on April 15, 1983—her ninety-first birthday.